Bowled Over

An Ashes Celebration

Bowled Over
An Ashes Celebration

My Side of the Story

STUART BROAD

with Paul Newman

HODDER &
STOUGHTON

To my family

First published in Great Britain in 2009 by Hodder & Stoughton
An Hachette UK company

1

Copyright © Stuart Broad 2009

A CIP catalogue record for this title is available from the British Library

Hardback ISBN 978 1 444 70476 1

Typeset in Fresco Sans

Printed and bound in Italy by L.E.G.O. Spa

Hodder & Stoughton policy is to use papers that are natural, renewable and
recyclable products and made from wood grown in sustainable forests. The logging
and manufacturing processes are expected to conform to the environmental
regulations of the country of origin.

Hodder & Stoughton Ltd
338 Euston Road
London NW1 3BH

www.hodder.co.uk

Contents

PART 1

Lighting the Fire

1 | Following in Dad's Footsteps

I guess I was born to be a cricketer. When my dad, the former England opening batsman Chris Broad, played for Nottinghamshire I would be down at Trent Bridge playing beyond the boundary with Phil Robinson, son of Dad's opening partner, Tim Robinson, and other kids of a very young age like myself.

Our pitch, so to speak, was underneath the old scoreboard and we used to play for hours and hours at a part of the ground that is now dominated by the new Radcliffe Road Stand, and there were even occasions when I followed my dad out on to the pitch as he was preparing to bat or field in the County Championship!

There was one occasion when Dad was walking out for his warm-up in his little tight shorts and wearing lots of gold chains, as was fashionable at the time, and I was just dragging my bat behind me as if I was going to warm up alongside him!

Then there was another time that Dad went out to bat after a lunch break and was taking guard and there I was wandering out to the middle as if I was going out to bat with him. I was carried off by someone and told to go and play out of harm's way. I could only have been about three or four years old.

I would also go into the changing rooms a few times, not as they are now because they've been changed around since those days, and on one occasion one of the Notts players – it was either Derek Randall or maybe Paul Johnson – hung me on a peg by my hoodie as they all went out to the field of play, leaving me dangling there for a while until someone came and rescued me. It seems I was part of the furniture and not averse to being the butt of the humour in the Notts dressing room.

Then, when Dad moved down to Bristol to play for Gloucestershire, I would spend a lot of time at the County Ground at Nevil Road playing with Phil Bainbridge's son and enjoying every moment of being around Dad and the other cricketers.

PREVIOUS PAGES: I was born to be a cricketer. Here I am, the budding all-rounder, following my dad Chris on to the field at Trent Bridge.

Courtney Walsh, then an overseas player for Gloucestershire, was someone I particularly liked and came to admire in those days because he would always be so nice to me when I was on one of my trips to Bristol to see Dad. I had no real idea then how good he was or what his immense achievements were. He was just such a nice man that I followed him as a hero and a legend throughout my teenage years. He would always throw me a ball and have time for me when he did not really need to.

The thing was, I didn't play any club cricket, certainly not until I was at least 11, because I was too busy enjoying the game being around Dad and in the back garden, where I would play for hours. That's where my love for the game was nurtured.

It may even sound a little bit sad now, but I used to play Test matches in my back garden. I would create scenarios that occurred during various

RIGHT: Dad was a stylish and successful batsman for England, or so he always tells me! Here he is displaying the stroke-making that made him an Ashes winner.

matches and act them out with my friend Mark Collier, who lived next door and was son of the now chief executive of the England and Wales Cricket Board, David Collier.

We would spend every day of the summer holidays at each other's houses, first playing a bit of cricket, then watching a bit of whatever Test match was going on at the time on TV, and would then go back into the garden and re-enact what we had just seen. This happened all day every day during the school holidays.

I would never pretend to be my dad during these epic made-up battles but they would usually involve England taking on Australia and I would often, as a left-handed batsman, end up being Matthew Hayden when it was my turn to be Australia.

If it was that time in the game when Australia would introduce their star leg-spinner, I would pretend to be Shane Warne and go through my overs trying to bowl leg-spin just like him. It was awesome and, funny as it might sound, these games helped me a lot as a player because I wasn't afraid to experiment as a bowler or batsman, and I certainly wasn't afraid of getting out, so I played with a freedom that can only have been good for my game. It was like getting into the right mindset at a young age. Neither of us boys liked losing, and it could be pretty intense, but, again, it was mainly about fun.

ABOVE LEFT: Here I am, aged four, displaying one of those flicks off the hips that my dad was so fond of, and now I am too.

ABOVE RIGHT: Getting in some early batting practice in the garden with my older sister Gemma, an accomplished wicket-keeper, who was always ready to pounce on any mistakes.

The legacy of those games was that I was never afraid to try something new in my professional career either, and that is quite a big thing really, because a lot of players might be apprehensive about attempting something that is alien to them.

I have always been a competitive sportsman. That old saying about the main point of any game being the taking part rather than the winning is rubbish as far as I'm concerned. I don't like that philosophy at all. For me it's all about winning because winning makes any game enjoyable, and that goes for any achievement, from winning an age group event with Leicestershire to winning the Ashes. They were both special as far as I was concerned because they were about coming out on top. There is no enjoyment in losing, no fun in taking consolation from being part of a great series or having a hand in a losing spectacle. Not if the outcome is the wrong one at the end of the day.

Some people have said that makes me a chip off the old block because my dad was very competitive throughout his career, but it came as much from my mum, Carole, as it did from Dad. Mum was competitive in a very positive way and I have to give her so much credit and thanks for encouraging me to achieve what I have gone on to do in cricket.

There were times as a kid when I would come home from school and go into the garden to practise my catching in the net that we had in the back. Mum would be cooking dinner, but would take a break from the

BELOW LEFT: You can see I am proud as punch at receiving a new Duncan Fearnley cricket bat, just like Dad's.

BELOW RIGHT: Proudly displaying my trophy as Melton rugby club's player of the year around the age of nine or ten.

kitchen to come outside and give me ten high catches that I would be galloping round the garden to collect. Little things like that meant the world to me.

I have so much respect for any parent who supports a sports-mad child: Mum would drive me all over the place to my games after she and Dad divorced, spending hours on giving me every encouragement possible.

It is the parents' Saturdays and Sundays, quite often their only break of the week from work, and they get in a car and spend the whole day supporting their children in whatever they want to do. In my case it would be games all over the place, and while I was playing, Mum would be there in her deckchair watching, enjoying talking to the other parents. And when I got in the car on the way home she was exactly the same whether I'd had a good or a bad day. She would just ask me if I had enjoyed the match and that was all she wanted me to do. After that she would change the subject and ask me what I wanted for dinner. There was no 'That was a rubbish shot' or 'Why did you bowl like that?' – the sort of stuff you might get from pushy parents.

This meant I was never upset at the end of a game, even if I'd played badly, and however competitive I was, Mum encouraged me to keep everything in perspective. Dad was the one who had a big hand in me playing cricket, and I admired him and the way he played the game, but it was my mum who really developed me as a character and was the one who was always there for me.

I was certainly never pushed into cricket by Dad, nor taken to any of his games by him to watch, play or learn. I would have my cut-down Duncan Fearnley Magnum bat, because they sponsored Dad, and that would go absolutely everywhere with me, but I didn't really play any organised cricket until I was almost in my teens.

My interest wasn't just cricket, even though that was undoubtedly my first sporting love. I played football, of course, but was more into hockey from the ages of 12 to 17, when I played representative games in the Midlands and had trials for the England age group sides. For a while I enjoyed playing hockey even more than I did cricket, perhaps around the time when I wasn't really being encouraged to bowl for Leicestershire age group teams.

I got a bit frustrated with my cricket when I was about 17 and was left out of a Leicestershire squad, and I told my mum that I was not really enjoying my cricket any more. Mum's answer was simple – don't play the game if you're not enjoying it. I don't think I ever seriously considered packing the game up, but I definitely didn't enjoy life in the age group set-

ABOVE LEFT: My passion for horse-riding came to an abrupt end when a pony bucked me off – never again!

ABOVE RIGHT: Here I am as a youngster enjoying one of my other sporting passions – rugby – and hitting a penalty through the posts. I'm still a Leicester Tigers supporter!

up at Leicestershire at that stage. Hockey, meanwhile, was really taking off for me and I was enjoying it both as a game and for the characters involved in it. Thankfully, it was a phase that I came through and I was soon loving my cricket as much as ever.

There is one important point to emphasise here. The game was all about fun throughout my childhood and I really believe that is how it should be. My parents were always full of encouragement without forcing me into anything or trying to maximise my potential, and that to me is the most productive way to get the best out of any promising sporting youngster.

It was about spontaneity rather than regimentation as far as I was concerned. There were no set guidelines. I would call up a friend to have a game in the garden and we would set up a big football net behind the batsman to be our wicketkeeper. Much better, I feel, than my dad ordering me down to the nets at a certain time with my gear to put me through my paces. Through trial and error I learnt more in the garden than I did in structured games of cricket. There was no fear of failure or fear of letting anyone down by getting out or bowling badly, and I think that stood me in good stead when I was older and making my way in the game.

At my club side, too, as I got older we would have a drink after games and talk about cricket, which was a fabulous way to learn. The adults would be there with their pints while we would stand around with our soft drinks, and I really think that was an important part of my sporting upbringing. You play better when you are enjoying yourself.

I would always arrive at a ground early if I was playing a game, but I would often find some other kid there before me having throwdowns with his dad, and even at a young age it would strike me that if practice was so regimented, it would probably not bring the best out of the youngster concerned.

I have always been naturally right-handed in that I have always written with my right hand, bowled right-handed and played both tennis and hockey right-handed. But I have always batted left-handed. People who don't follow cricket find that a bit hard to understand and can find it strange, but it has always been natural to me, not least because it means my stronger hand, my right one, is on the top of the handle when I bat. With my technique that really helps me.

In my younger days I was mainly a batsman, and not a particularly good one at that. I was quite small until I was about 16, when suddenly I shot up about a foot in height, and I used to get pretty dull thirties because I was solid enough but didn't have the strength to be expansive.

Perhaps I started to realise that I might be quite good at cricket when I was 17 and had a remarkable summer. I think I scored about eight hundreds in seven weeks for various teams, ranging from my club side to the Leicestershire Under 17s, and I think that changed my attitude towards the game because it gave me a lot of confidence.

I had always been a bowler as well as a batsman for my school side, Oakham in Leicestershire, because the masters of cricket there, the former England batsmen Frank Hayes and David Steele, thought I could bowl and

A lovely straight hit down the fairway – a shot I haven't always been able to repeat in recent years as golf practice has to take second place to cricket.

With Gemma in our garden just after leaving Oakham School. Now we are both representing our country, me playing for England, and Gemma as our team computer analyst, looking at our performances and the opposition's.

encouraged me. So much so that they would become frustrated on my behalf because at that stage Leicestershire would not give me a bowl and they felt that I deserved one. It was not so much the age group coaches but my captains at that time, who, if you think about it, get a lot of responsibility at such a young age by deciding who bats where and who bowls.

Mind you, that did not do me any harm in the long term because it meant I did not do too much bowling in my younger years and perhaps I am feeling the benefits of that now. My body had time to develop between 14 and 17 without the stresses of fast bowling on it, and it was only when I was stronger that I began to really develop as a bowler.

During that time when I was flirting with concentrating on hockey rather than cricket, I was left out of a Leicestershire group side but got called up because of an injury for a game against Derbyshire.

I opened the batting and got 197 in a two-day game on a flat wicket, and when we were struggling to bowl Derbyshire out I was thrown the ball as something of a last resort. But I got four wickets in next to no time and I think Leicestershire realised I could bowl after that. They were like: 'Oh, you can bowl after all.' I quickly told them that I had been bowling for my school for the last three years and had always wanted to be both a batsman and a bowler. At the end of that game I was invited to the Leicestershire academy and things went from there really.

At the age of 17 I played in my first second-team game for Leicestershire, got a contract at the end of that season and went to Australia, where I bowled throughout that winter. Finally, I was getting somewhere while still thoroughly enjoying myself.

Going to Australia to further my cricketing development was a huge time for me both as a cricketer and as a person. I had left home and gone to Australia, which is quite a tough place to go to at such a young age, but the guys I played with were fantastic to me.

I opened both the batting and the bowling for a six-month period for Hoppers Crossing in Melbourne sub-district cricket, and it was drilled into me that I could never miss a practice on either a Tuesday or a Thursday if I expected to play for the club at weekends.

That disciplined approach paid off for me because whenever they needed a wicket they would throw the ball to me, which had never happened to me in my life because even at school, where they believed in my bowling, I was more of a dibbly-dobbly merchant than a strike bowler. Now I was being encouraged to charge in and I wasn't held back by any restriction on the amount of overs I could bowl at such a young age, as happens in England.

I was bowling 20 overs a day, including ten-over spells on occasion, and because I only did it for a six-month period rather than the whole year round, and because I had not been overbowled throughout my youth, my body could cope with it.

It actually helped me get stronger and enabled me to learn how to bowl on flat wickets for long spells in games that were real battles. Remember I was used to public school cricket at Oakham, which was all well and good and nice to play in, but the bowlers would pitch it up to you when you were batting and it was all very pleasant.

Australian cricket, meanwhile, was tough. I was called all sorts of things, and there were people sledging me, swearing at me and in my face all the time, and it got me used to being in a real battle. I had never been used to anything like it before.

Over that winter I had grown a lot, and even though I had been signed on my first contract with Leicestershire as a batting all-rounder, from the moment I first practised in the nets as a contracted player, I was suddenly swinging the ball as a bowler from a taller height and it was bouncing from a better length.

The nets were a little bit juicy because it was pre-season, but I was getting the ball to talk. I remember Darren Maddy, one of the senior Leicestershire players, telling people how I had improved dramatically. Even though I was still in awe of all these players in the first team, I played only two more second-team games to add to the one I had played the previous summer when I was handed my first-class debut.

It all happened extremely quickly, which again gave me no time to fear anything. I got looked after very well at this stage in my career, and the development of me from the time I broke into the Leicestershire first-team squad, by people like James Whitaker, H.D. Ackerman and Ottis Gibson, was sublime. They only played me in Championship cricket so as not to rush me, while, even though he was the senior bowler in the side, Ottis would run into the wind or uphill to allow me to have any benefits and advantages that the conditions could offer. An amazing gesture to a young bowler when you come to think about it. Anything anyone at the club could do to help me as a young bowler, which was what I had become, was never any trouble for them.

And they were very clever in giving me my first-team Championship debut in a game staged at Oakham School, where I was educated and which I knew so well. It was the start of my professional journey, one that was to take me to the very top with England.

The newly professional Stuart Broad making my career here at Grace Road with Leicestershire. I owe my first county an awful lot.

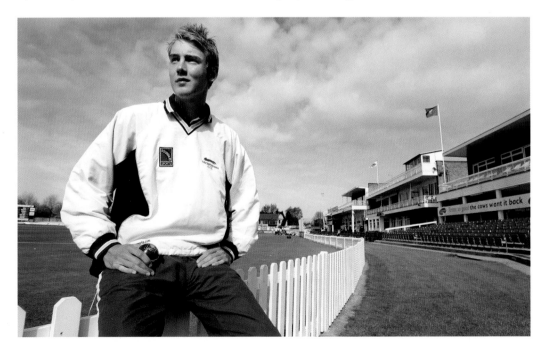

2 | Making My Way

Oakham School in Leicestershire was an amazing place for me both academically and in terms of my cricket. But you can have the best facilities in the world yet all that really matters is the personnel within them, and in Frank Hayes and David Steele I had the perfect people to guide my young cricketing career.

They have finished now, but you could not have two better cricket masters for any young player to learn the rudiments of the game. Frank played for Lancashire and England, while David was one of Northants' finest and was also once the BBC Sports Personality of the Year after his own heroics in an England shirt.

Again, win or lose, you would leave any game smiling, which is exactly how it should be. People might look at my competitive nature and think it strange that I should feel that way, but it is vital as a sportsman that you do not get too high after a victory or too low after a defeat. Keeping the balance right, treating the twin impostors of triumph and disaster the same, is the key ingredient for any successful sportsman.

Winning is everything to me, as I have said, but whenever we lost at Oakham, Frank and David would come into the changing room and tell us a story of a game they once lost, an important game, a Test match, but then they went out for a beer, talked about it and life would not seem quite so bad.

We would walk round the ground in their company during the matches for hours, hanging on to everything they said and intrigued by the words of wisdom they bestowed on us at regular intervals. I would be batting in a game, look up and see some of the other boys walking around with David, listening to what he had to say about the game.

Steeley is an accomplished after-dinner speaker, and he would leave us all spellbound with his stories about the game and the characters in it both in his day and in other eras. There was an occasion when one of the lads got hit by a ball on his inner thigh and immediately a big lump came up. He felt sore and was worried about going out to bat again, and how the affect of this blow might hinder him. But Steeley just said: 'Rub it for ten seconds and it will be gone by the time you come back from your innings.' We would believe anything he said, so this lad did what he was told, rubbed it and was convinced that it had made all the difference. The man was like a magician to us, capable of anything.

It was more of a club atmosphere than a school environment and that was marvellous to us. The groundsman, Keith Exton, who has now gone on to be the groundsman at the Swalec Stadium in Cardiff, was also an absolute hero to all of us players. Normally, groundsmen are so protective of their facilities and cautious about anybody using them when they do not need to, but if ever we wanted a cheeky net after chemistry lessons, for example, Keith would do us proud.

He would prepare us a quick wicket on the other side of the playing field so that the teachers wouldn't see us and off we would go! You do not normally get this in a school, but in our final year we were so close to our teachers that we would go for drinks with them after a game. It was such a lovely environment that we would be trained to talk for hours about cricket as a team, the players and the staff and the groundsman. It was quite superb.

Taking my early steps as a professional for Leicestershire after learning my cricket in the county at Oakham School.

It was one of the things that Peter Moores was big on when he was England coach. He would tell us about how the game has changed, how

players didn't meet up after a game nearly so much now, just to talk over a drink, young and old.

I guess it is the price of progress in some ways. Cricketers are more likely to be fitter athletes these days and as a consequence do not sit in the bar after a match discussing cricket over a pint. It's what they used to do and it's where countless players learnt so much about the game from their elders. We should do more of it now, not necessarily over a pint, but just making sure we talk. It's good to talk.

When I did it I would spend hours with these guys talking cricket, with a Coca-Cola in my hand while they had their beer, and if I was to tell a young player making his way anything, it would be this. Enjoy yourself but also do not be afraid to make mistakes through trial and error because it is the best way to learn. Develop your game and then talk about it with your seniors because that is how you get better.

I could have a bad day after a school match at Oakham and then David or Frank would talk to me, remind me about the jaffa I bowled to get a wicket. I would forget about all the things that went wrong and suddenly I would feel that life wasn't so bad after all.

I have carried that through my career because, even at this relatively early stage of my time in cricket, I have still had huge ups and downs. But I try to stay somewhere around the middle, keeping it all in context. If I have a bad day I'm down, but I do not go to my hotel room and beat myself up about it; and conversely, if I have a fantastic day I do not get too high. Staying on a level platform is the key.

Yes, I know I can be hotheaded on the field, and I know I can kick the turf when things go wrong, but that is just me in my bowling bubble – fired up and wanting to get people out. But once I leave the changing room, I might talk about what's happened during the day, but I will not dwell on the things I have done.

My philosophy is simple. Do not have any regrets. Play the game with everything you have got on any particular day and then, if it is not good enough, forget about it and move on.

To illustrate my point: Mushtaq Ahmed being in the England dressing room is absolutely huge for me and everyone within the set-up. He is such an amazing character. He believes in playing with flair, without worrying about the consequences, and he has become an immensely important figure in moving our team forward.

Mushtaq was recruited as a spin coach but has become so much more than that to so many of us, and he is really missed when he is not in the

ABOVE LEFT: Tim Boon (*right*) has been a fantastic coach for Leicestershire after joining them from the England set-up, and he did a lot for me while I was with the county.

TOP RIGHT: My dad Chris (*left*) has always been a big influence on me without being a pushy or over-competitive parent.

BOTTOM RIGHT: Individual awards are a satisfying part of cricket, but it's playing in a winning team that counts.

England dressing room. He is such a good man to talk to that it is the equivalent of having a chat about the game over a pint at the end of a day's play.

As that is not really the done thing these days, I will sit with Mushtaq on the balcony or in the dressing room for the first session of a day's play in a Test if we are batting and just talk and talk and talk. I always learn so much from our chats.

So when I made my first-class debut at Oakham School for Leicestershire against Somerset in 2005 I felt very much at home. I got Michael Burns out in both innings, but quite a weird trend in my career was followed in that match. In any debut I have ever had in any form of cricket I have only ever got one wicket in the innings, which is quite odd really, but it was something that happened as well against Somerset.

I was playing against the likes of Sanath Jayasuriya and Graeme Smith, who were both playing for Somerset at that time, and it was an amazing experience to be at my old school, with everyone I knew around me, playing in what was the biggest match I had experienced up until that point. I had only played at Grace Road, the headquarters of Leicestershire cricket, twice by that stage.

I played in eight Championship games in 2005, and played against the Australians, but 2006 was my breakthrough year, as it were. I played a lot more cricket, took more than 50 Championship wickets and played a bit of one-day cricket.

But it was our Twenty20 campaign that really brought me to the attention of a wider cricketing world. We had a brilliant approach to the short form of the game that was to win us the Twenty20 Cup, and it was one I was delighted to play a part in.

We had a great team and an attack that was based on Dinesh Mongia, Claude Henderson and Jeremy Snape all bowling spin, while I was given licence to attack at the head of our opponents' innings.

In every game I was told to bowl my four overs at the top of the innings to try to take wickets, whatever the cost, and my way of trying to take wickets was to bang out a good length, particularly at Grace Road. People would think that 160 or 170 was a good Twenty20 score at that stage in England, but at our home ground we were confident of defending 120 or 130. We could always win if we had 130 on the board, and throughout that season I ended up going at an economy rate of 4.2 an over for the whole tournament, which, in Twenty20, I had to be happy with. And I did it without bowling one slower ball or bouncer. It was all about consistency then.

The Twenty20 Cup that year gave me my first experience of big crowds and great atmospheres. We would play in front of sell-outs at Grace Road, and while crowds of 5,000 might not sound that much, they would create a fabulous atmosphere, one that a young cricketer like myself would revel in and hopefully thrive on.

It came to finals day at Trent Bridge, where I had spent so much time playing beyond the boundary while my dad was starring for Notts, and an encounter in our semi-final against Essex was to show many people, including myself, that I had a chance of making it on the big stage.

I had quite a big battle with Ronnie Irani, at that stage the Essex captain and one of the most destructive one-day batsmen in the country, and it was him who to a large extent stood between us and a place in the final of what was becoming the biggest domestic limited-overs competition.

I had watched Ronnie playing for England while I was growing up, and he was someone who I was acutely aware represented a huge risk to us.

He was a big character who was not afraid to be aggressive on the cricket field, and when I stared at him, as I was wont to do even at that stage of my career, he stared at me.

He said to me: 'You're as big an idiot as your dad was,' and I replied that he was old enough to have played against both of us so he would know. That got Ronnie going again, but he couldn't get my bowling away, which was a huge encouragement for both me and Leicestershire.

We had talked about him before the game, and Paul Nixon, one of the most impressive characters it has been my pleasure to play with, came up to me and said: 'Whatever you do, make sure Irani doesn't hit you back over your head. That's where he is strong.'

So every ball, as I ran in, I was saying to myself: 'Make sure he can't hit you back over your head', and as a consequence I was bowling deliveries that were hitting his splice and he couldn't get away. In the end he got a nine-ball duck after he had been niggling at everybody in our side, not just me, and when he was out everybody sprinted up to me, giving him a send-off, and it was terrific. It was actually one of the best feelings I have ever had after taking a wicket.

Making an impact on a big, televised occasion is very good for a young cricketer. It is why I am happy to see the likes of Joe Denly in the England side now as I write this. Every time I have seen him in a televised match for Kent he has done well, and that says something for a player's big-match temperament.

So that Twenty20 Cup finals day was a big stepping stone for me as a player. It was the biggest occasion I had played in at that time and I had managed to succeed, we had gone on to win it, and suddenly I was being talked of as a possible candidate for the final Test squad of that summer, which was being named the following weekend.

I was thinking then, when I saw my name in the papers as an England possibility: 'No way, there's no way England will pick me at this stage', but by the end of that season I was playing for my country in the one-day series against Pakistan.

I was actually picked on my Twenty20 and Championship form because my one-day international debut for England was actually only my fourth professional game over 50 overs. I held my own, getting a few wickets here and there, but I came up against a formidable Pakistan side and I was quickly made aware that I was making quite a big step up for one so young.

It was also around this time that people were making me aware just how similar my batting style was to my dad's. Now, it really must be in the

Facing the press is part of an England player's job after both good games and bad. Here I am pondering the next question.

We used to enjoy our off-duty games of rugby and cricket before injuries put a stop to our fun. Here I am showing Michael Yardy a clean pair of heels.

genes because it is something I have never actually worked on and I have never tried to emulate my dad at any stage.

Yes, I talked to my dad about my batting, but in fact I was never coached by him and it was only a bit later on, when I was trying to improve my batting at the highest level, that he talked to me extensively about it to give me a template of how to bat for England.

For instance, since my discussions with Dad, I will never try to pull any ball now before I have reached 20 in any innings. He has encouraged me to leave outside off stump in the early part of my innings. He has tried to turn my thought processes into a batsman's in recent years, but it is not something we ever concentrated on when I was young. The clips and punches, the shots that my dad was famous for as a left-handed opening batsman for England, are shots that come naturally to me too.

Not that I didn't have the opportunity to see how my dad earned his success as the star of England's Ashes-winning series in Australia in 1986-7. I used to joke with him that whenever I went round to his house he would have the video of the highlights on, or the video perched on top of the pile he had by the side of his video recorder.

In all seriousness, I was obviously very proud of what Dad achieved but I also watched those tapes to have a close look at the England bowlers and their approaches. I would watch Phillip DeFreitas, all whirling arms and legs, and I would watch Gladstone Small, Graham Dilley and the rest. It was a great series after all, and England haven't managed to win in Australia since – yet – so it was a series I watched a lot as a kid, not just as the proud son of a successful father.

I also had to make a big decision around this time. I left Leicestershire – where I had grown up, where I had convinced them that I could bowl, and where I had made my name – for Nottinghamshire.

I owe an awful lot to Leicestershire. I had not set the world alight when I was with them, and it is conceivable that if I had been with a bigger club, I might have fallen by the wayside before I had the chance to be an England cricketer.

They had seen something in me and they had supported me in fulfilling my potential, not least in giving me my chance in Championship cricket before I had even taken a 'five-for' for the second team.

Leicestershire was a huge stepping stone for me, I loved playing for them and I was proud to be a full Leicestershire player for two seasons, but I was not sure where the club was going.

Tim Boon, the Leicestershire coach, is one of the great men of cricket, and I sat down with him and Neil Davidson, the chairman of the club, to discuss my future. I had already made up my mind to leave for Notts, and I wanted to tell them on my own without the help of my agent, but I was nervous about breaking the news.

Tim, who had been in the international set-up as an assistant coach and had groomed me for what was necessary, fully understood my decision. I felt that it was crucial for me to play first-division cricket because I was beginning to see quite a difference in standards between that and what I was experiencing in division two at Leicester.

I was playing one-day international cricket with England, and my gut instinct was that I needed to play at a higher level of domestic cricket to help my international chances. Another part of the appeal of Notts was that I would be playing at a Test match ground because the Leicester wicket was not very special and I would be surrounded by big players at Trent Bridge like Chris Read, Ryan Sidebottom, Graeme Swann and Mark Ealham.

I knew that Mick Newell and Paul Johnson were part of a very good set-up at Notts, and I thought it would be the best place for me to progress my career.

Leicestershire never actually offered me a new contract. They just seemed to accept that I was going. They never came to me and said: 'Look, this is where we are going and we want you to be a leading part in it.'

I was angry, in fact, at Neil Davidson because he came out in the

A satisfying wicket. Dismissing Yuvraj Singh (*right*) has been particularly sweet ever since he hit me for six sixes in an over in Durban.

ABOVE LEFT: You have to treat failure and success just the same. Here I congratulate Yuvraj after his heroics against me in the 2007 World Twenty20.

ABOVE RIGHT: The great South African Allan Donald (*left*) was the England bowling coach when I made my debut in 2006.

Leicester Mercury and said that I had only left for the money, which was an absolute load of rubbish. I don't want Leicestershire fans to think that because it is not true.

I went to play first-division cricket at a Test match ground on a better wicket with better players around me to guide me and help me develop. I was not in the Test match side at that time and that was my absolute aim, to play Test cricket for England. It is still my aim. So I had to make a move to try to give myself the best chance of making that happen.

I owe a lot to people like James Whitaker, Tim Boon and Paul Nixon, the perfect man to start your Test career with. Nicko gave me a lot of my views as to how I want to play my cricket and I was very fortunate to play some of my formative years with him because he is such a great character. But even Nicko wasn't going to be around for ever, and I had to think of my future. I moved on, but my immediate future, I am happy to say, was to be dominated by England.

3 | An England Player

I held my own when I first became an England player, taking a few wickets against a Pakistan side that boasted excellent players such as Inzamam-ul-Haq, Mohammad Yousuf and Younis Khan. It was tough but it was a great experience.

My role in the team had also changed substantially from those days in Leicestershire age group cricket, when I was primarily a batsman whose bowling was not trusted. Now I was a frontline seamer and, for England, a number 11 batsman.

I think I averaged nine in my first season of full county cricket because I had never batted at numbers 10 or 11 before, so when I came in I thought I had to play shots from the start and would invariably nick the ball straight away.

The year I was picked for England, 2006, my cricket had improved to the point where I had scored a couple of fifties but I was finding batting a whole new experience. People like Andrew Caddick would be hurling the ball past my nose, and I was thinking: 'Where am I even going to hit the ball, let alone score?' I knew I had to sort my batting out, but I also felt it was probably a case of adjusting to the higher standards and adapting accordingly. The change, after all, was stark. I had gone from facing 70 miles per hour bowling on a length at school to 85 miles an hour from Caddick past my nose.

It took me 18 months to find a technique to cope with that, and 2007 saw me average 30-odd with the bat and made me realise that I was capable of scoring hundreds at county level. And if I could do it there, I felt I could develop into a more than useful batsman for England because, odd though it might sound, I think I have a batting technique suited to Test cricket.

By that I mean the wickets are flat, generally, in Test cricket and the ball does not move around substantially. Okay, the bowlers are quicker and better, but you can hit through the line, and someone like me, who likes to punch off the back foot, can hang back in Test cricket and hopefully prosper. It certainly suits me more than having to come forward on slow, seaming pitches with the ball moving around a lot more.

There was speculation that I was going to make my Test debut in the first match of the 2007 series against India. I had been doing well in the

Championship and in one-day cricket for England, and people were beginning to suggest that I was ready for the ultimate form of the game, even though I think the England management had some concerns about whether I was physically ready.

I played for the England Lions against India ahead of the first Test and had taken five wickets in an innings and hit a fifty, which earned me selection in the squad for the first Test, and it was then a question of whether I would make the final cut.

It really looked as if I was going to play, which was an unbelievable feeling, but the day before the game Peter Moores, the England coach, came up to me and said they were going to go with Chris Tremlett, who had been brought into the squad as a replacement for the injured Steve Harmison. I was absolutely devastated.

It remains the hardest thing I have ever done to leave that England dressing room carrying my bags away from Lord's having not been picked. It was heartbreaking, but what I did do well after that setback and throughout that summer was to go back and perform in county cricket whenever I was left out of a Test team. The danger when you are on the fringes of selection is that you go off the boil, your level of performance in county

A very proud moment, receiving my England Test cap from captain Michael Vaughan ahead of my debut against Sri Lanka in Colombo.

cricket declines and you are quickly forgotten by England. I had to keep knocking on the door.

Then I did well on the one-day leg of our tour to Sri Lanka towards the end of 2007, another big time in my development because I started to experiment more as a bowler. We had lost the first match of the 50-over series in Dambulla and had looked quite limited as an attack in Sri Lankan conditions, when Peter Moores came up to me and said: 'Have you got a leg-cutter?' I said I hadn't and he urged me to try it, but it is fair to say it did not go well initially, my first three deliveries in practice hitting the side netting rather than going anywhere near the stumps.

Peter urged me to keep trying, and by the end of that series it was my best ball and I class that now as one of my best deliveries when I am trying to tie up a batsman. I owe Mooresey and Ottis Gibson, my old Leicestershire team-mate and by this time the England bowling coach, an awful lot for that. It was summed up for me by the final ball I bowled in that series as we wrapped up a significant one-day series win. It was a leg-cutter that came out perfectly to dismiss the batsman, and while he was only a number 11, it was a very satisfying moment, the ball pitching on middle and leg and hitting the top of off. As I walked off, Mooresey had the biggest smile on his face, as if to say: 'That's perfect, you've nailed it.' His making me try that ball and helping me was really good coaching.

My big moment, my Test debut, finally came late in 2007 on tour in Sri Lanka, in Colombo, at a time when we had a number of injuries to people

Kevin Pietersen (*left*) is a magnificent batsman and a key member of our side. He was missed during the second half of the Ashes series.

like Matthew Hoggard and Jimmy Anderson. It wasn't exactly the venue you would dream about making your debut at as a bowler, being both very flat and very hot, but it turned out to be a good Test for me. I bowled 36 overs against some of the best batsmen in the world, taking my customary one wicket on a debut, and it was quite a respectable return in very tough conditions.

I remember when Mahela Jayawardene, then the Sri Lankan captain, came out to bat and a list of his highest Test scores came up on the big screen at the Sinhalese Sports Club ground. It was like 300-odd, 270-odd and lots more like it – and they all seemed to have been scored in Colombo. I was like: 'Oh, no!' Of course, he went on to another double hundred against us, but all in all it was a step up that I was pleased with.

I was left out of the rest of that series, but my big Test breakthrough came in New Zealand during the second tour of that 2007–8 winter, when

Playing a shot through the covers that Dad would have been proud of. Must be something in the genes.

I played and got crucial wickets and runs after missing the first Test of the series, in Hamilton, which we lost.

We came back to win in both Wellington and Napier to win the series and it was a phenomenal feeling to be part of that. I remember watching the first Test of that series and thinking we were low on confidence and it showed in the way we played. I was determined to try to do my bit to put that right when Jimmy and I came in at Wellington. When I got two wickets in an over in the second innings I was running around madly and

Michael Vaughan, our captain, said afterwards that that was the kind of enthusiasm he was looking for. It was lovely to hear.

I loved the whole atmosphere of Test cricket. The Barmy Army, as always, were out in force, and I went on to have what I consider still to be one of my best Test matches in Napier, which is renowned for its batsman-friendly conditions. It's a really flat wicket, there are short boundaries, and even though it was 1–1 in the series, we really needed to win because it was a series we were expected to win and win well.

We were in difficulties at first but Kevin Pietersen got a century and I played a part in a big partnership with him with my first meaningful innings for England. Then, after New Zealand got off to a flyer, myself and Ryan Sidebottom came into the attack and bowled them out in a session. Ryan took seven wickets, I took three and I was absolutely delighted to make a contribution, particularly as I bowled 17 overs on the bounce. Then second time round I got runs and wickets again, and it was a very important game in proving to myself that I could take wickets on flat pitches. I realised that I can do it and I will do it.

I moved to Notts to further my ambitions in cricket, not for money, as some at Leicestershire claimed.

I have made steady progress since then. I know, at this still relatively early stage of my career, that I owe an awful lot to the coaches and captains who have put so much faith in me. I have had Tests where I have not taken a wicket, but they have stuck by me and that has been hugely important to my development.

I reckon if I had played in the 1980s, when there was little selectorial continuity, that I would only have played five or six Tests by now because I would have played a couple and been dropped and then the same thing would have happened again. But England have stuck with me because they have seen something in me, and it has been up to me to justify the belief that people have had in me.

There have been a few setbacks along the way but I hope I have proved I can recover from them pretty quickly. For instance, there was the time in the first World Twenty20 tournament in South Africa when Yuvraj Singh hit me for six sixes in an over. And there was the disappointment of defeat by Holland in the second World Twenty20 at Lord's, when I missed a couple of runout chances to win the match in the last over. But the key is how you react to things like that, and I like to think I have reacted positively when adversity has come my way.

I think it comes down to what I have said about keeping the highs and lows in perspective. I tend to dissect a performance to see what I could have done better because improvement is all about trial and error.

What happens happens and what's done is done, but you can always learn from things. If I have a bad day, by the time I wake up the next morning, it's gone and I have to refocus on what I'm doing.

I joined Nottinghamshire because they are a big, ambitious, first division county who play at a Test ground. And it feels like home. On the balcony (*left–right*) are me, Paul Franks, Darren Pattinson, Andy Carter and Will Jefferson.

The World Twenty20 defeat by Holland could have been avoided if I had executed one of my runout chances in the final over.

The Holland game was a case in point. They didn't need too many from that last over, so they started off as favourites, really, but I missed those runout chances and the game was gone. But what that meant to me was that I had to bounce back against Pakistan in the next match, and I turned out to be one of our most successful bowlers in that tournament.

I never sit in my room and nail myself. I am a positive person and I am fully aware that in international sport you are going to have massive ups and downs.

The Yuvraj over was a wake-up call to me because I was a young lad who had bowled length in county cricket all the time and that incident made me appreciate that I had to learn new skills if I was to prosper as a bowler for England.

There has been drama and turmoil too in my relatively short time with England building up to the 2009 Ashes. The winter of 2008–9 had just about everything that international sport can offer.

We had beaten South Africa well in the one-day series of 2008 under Kevin Pietersen but then we had a very unsettled winter, beginning with our match in Antigua against the 'Stanford Superstars' for a prize of $20 million.

The Stanford experience was a strange one for the team. It wasn't so much a cricket match as a show, and my view is that we should never have gone there as the England cricket team. We should have been the Lions Superstars or something like that to try to emphasise that this was not an official match for England, one that should have been played with us wearing the three lions on our chests.

The thing was we were not playing against another Test nation, but a team bearing Sir Allen Stanford's name, and many of us felt uncomfortable about being put in that position. Anything that Stanford wanted we had to do because he was paying so much money for us to be there, and the experience wasn't made any better for me by my being ill and confined to bed for three or four days in Antigua.

Then we went straight to India for our full tour there, where we slipped to a 5–0 deficit in the seven-match one-day series before the terrorist attacks on Mumbai brought an abrupt, albeit temporary, halt to our trip.

It was a difficult time. There was the whole question after the attacks of whether we were going home, and we were holed up in our hotel with massive security surrounding us, partly because we were in the same hotel as the Indian team and some threats had been made against them too.

Then the decision was made for us to go home for a while and the feeling among the boys at that stage was that there was no way we would be returning to India for the Test series after what had happened.

Then, when we were at home, the call was made that we would return to India, initially via a holding camp in Abu Dhabi, and, to be fair, we never felt in any danger when we played our two-Test series in India and we were very well looked after.

Admittedly, it was still a very hard three weeks because we were not allowed to leave our hotel rooms when we were not either playing or practising, which was quite tough. But we actually ended up playing some decent cricket on that tour before we were beaten by the better side.

We returned to India on the advice of our security expert, Reg Dickason, someone I would trust with my life. Reg is fantastically experienced in this field and has been through some situations in his life that most of us will never experience. But as a player and as a human being, I had big reservations about going back because what had happened in Mumbai had been truly shocking.

We had seen some pretty graphic television pictures of the terrorist attacks, and we were in the country where it had happened. We were seeing pictures of people being killed at the Taj Mahal Palace Hotel, and because we had stayed there it all seemed very close to home.

Just a few weeks earlier I had had a meal with my dad in the hotel restaurant where so many people were killed, and it's hard not to imagine yourself in that terrorist scenario and wondering if you are truly safe.

Security was tight during our one-day tour of India, even before the terrorist attacks on Mumbai. When we went back for the Test series it was tightened even more.

Most of the team had reservations about going back, but Reg's security report came in, steps were taken to make us as secure as possible, and back we went to try to win a Test series over there.

Then there was the even more shocking experience of the Sri Lankan cricket team being attacked by terrorists in Lahore in incidents that my dad, Chris, was caught up in as the ICC match referee for their series against Pakistan.

We were in Barbados during our West Indies tour and I had missed a phone call from my dad at 1 a.m. I woke up around 2 a.m. and noticed that I had missed a call, which seemed very strange to me because he knew what time it would have been in the Caribbean. I called him back and got no reply, so called my sister Gemma, who was in Australia. She had spoken to Dad and told me that he was in a bunker because there had been a bit of an incident which he didn't elaborate on. He just wanted us to know that he was safe and we should wait for him to get in touch again.

So I turned on my TV and there it was – a cricket team being attacked by gunmen. It shook me up but I was calmed down by the knowledge of Dad being okay. Then there was the thought of the wider picture and the implications of it. We knew the Sri Lankan players and were friends with them, and there they were having rocket launchers fired at them. I also discovered that my dad's driver had been killed and that Dad had been covering the wounds of another man who had been shot in his van.

It was just horrific and I do not think my dad will ever find his way back to Pakistan. There will certainly need to be a major improvement in security for touring teams in Pakistan before England could even begin to contemplate touring there again. It is a huge shame but it is just the way it is in the modern world.

Dad has recovered well from that experience, but the extent of what he went through became evident to me a few weeks after when I went with him to see an action film at the cinema.

The first scene saw a guy sprinting through the streets when suddenly a hitman came out and started shooting at him. I turned to Dad and saw him shaking. His face was completely white. I had never seen him like that.

I said: 'Are you all right, Dad?' He didn't say anything. Then I asked him again and he said: 'That was the exact sound of the bullets hitting our van.' Me being me I said: 'They got the sound effects right then!' and then he moved and was okay.

I had tried to make light of it, but it was a pretty shocking moment for Dad because it brought what had happened all back to him.

I think it was a disgrace how Dad was treated after that. They basically said that Dad's description of what happened was wrong. Well, I'm afraid *they* are wrong because I have seen the footage of what happened. There didn't seem to be any policemen around when the gunmen attacked, so I'm not sure the presidential-level security was working.

To be fair, maybe Dad feels now that he shouldn't have done a press conference so soon after the attacks, but at the end of the day people wanted to know what had happened and Dad is a very honest character. Some people didn't like the truth.

I know one thing. The whole business justified our decision not to go to Pakistan for the Champions Trophy in 2008. There had been a lot of pressure put on us too, with security people telling us everything would be fine and Haroon Lorgat of the International Cricket Council assuring us that we would be fine.

But Reg said we shouldn't go and he was spot on, which is why we trust Reg with everything.

Then, at the start of 2009, came the turmoil of losing both our captain, Kevin Pietersen, and coach, Peter Moores, because of a dispute between the pair of them. It came as a genuine shock because I did not have a clue there was a problem between them.

They seemed to get on well and team talks were good. I never saw any signs of stress or strain, so when it all came out in the press I couldn't believe it. We had phone calls from the ECB asking us for our views, and all I could honestly say was that I didn't have a problem with either of them.

I loved working with Peter Moores. He was one of the best coaches I worked with. And we had had success under KP, so it was all very difficult. But the team reacted very well to it all.

Glenn McGrath is the biggest role model for me, and I hope as I develop as a bowler that my style will be similar to his.

England v West Indies
Winners 2009

I always think you should enjoy the highs. Here we are celebrating beating the West Indies in the 2009 one-day series in England.

Andrew Strauss took over as captain and we had a big team meeting at Gatwick Airport prior to leaving for the West Indies soon after the pair of them had been replaced. The players sat down and said this is where we want the team to go and a big statement was, 'This is not a lease car, it's our own car, and we have to do things the way we want this team to go forward and buy into it.'

Okay, we lost the Test series against the West Indies, but we played some really good cricket there and I think it was the start of us building momentum that was to carry us through to the Ashes series.

My decision to turn down the opportunity to play in the Indian Premier League was a huge one for me. It was an opportunity to earn a lot of money and also, crucially, to gain high-quality experience of Twenty20 cricket against the very best players. But it was not right for me at that stage.

I made the decision when we were in St Kitts at the start of England's tour of the West Indies early in 2009. I had spoken with my mum and dad and my agent, Craig Sackfield, and at that stage I was not sure if I was going to be in the side for the Test series in the Caribbean.

Even then I was desperate to play in the Ashes series the following summer, it was the ultimate dream, and I felt that what I did at the start of Ashes year would have an impact on the rest of what was a huge summer.

My feeling was that, if I was fortunate enough to be picked for all the international matches on the Caribbean tour, I would have played four Tests and five one-day internationals before, if I accepted one of the three or four

IPL offers on the table for me, going to play there for three weeks and then heading immediately into our home return series against the West Indies.

There was just no way, at my age, that my body would have been able to do that. My dad straight away said: 'Don't go' when I talked about the IPL to him, and I agreed completely. I was 22, I have got a lot of cricket ahead of me and my sole aim in my career is to be successful for England. I want to play 100 Tests and I want to break one-day international records. I want to win more Ashes series and I want to win World Cups.

Let's be honest. If you play ten years for England, you will not be struggling financially, but money has never been by prime objective. That will come if I continue to do well. As far as the IPL was concerned, I knew it would be in my best interests to have a small break at that time rather than playing more cricket, particularly to try to restore a bit of mental freshness.

I had just bought a house and I saw that period as a great chance to spend some time in it and play a Championship match for Notts to make sure I was in that Test match side to face the West Indies at the start of the return tour by them.

I remembered what had happened in 2007 when the West Indies last toured. Ryan was brought into the team for the Test at Headingley, swung the ball round corners and went on to have a fantastic year, one that culminated with him becoming England's player of the year. A bowler had taken wickets at the start of a summer and had stayed in the side.

I knew I had to be in that first Test side because if it swung I would get wickets and would then be perfectly positioned to challenge for an Ashes place. If I had gone to the IPL, I wouldn't have had that little break, I wouldn't have taken seven wickets in a game for Notts and, you never know, I might not have been in the team for the first Test against the West Indies. And that would have left me playing catch-up.

Yes, there was some banter in the England dressing room when I said I was not going to the IPL. Some players said: 'Have you seen it? It's amazing. You've got to go', but I was like: 'I'm 22, hopefully I've got a lot of time ahead of me and I need to make sure I'm a decent England player first.'

Of course, I could fully understand other people wanting to go, particularly those at different stages of their career from me, but I was sure I had made the right decision. The level of backing I received, though, surprised me. The public were great and some of my closest friends said to me: 'Great decision, really respect you for that.'

As it turned out, it was perfect because it kept me fresh for the whole of the Ashes series. And that was to be the series that changed my life.

PART 2

The Ashes
2009

4 | First Test
The Big Day Dawns in Cardiff

As a bowler you always have to be in form because there is a lot of depth in England and there is always someone challenging for your place. You are only one game away from another bowler taking six wickets in a Championship match and being under the spotlight, with people saying he deserves an England place.

So I knew I had to keep taking wickets to fulfil my dream of playing in the 2009 Ashes series. The World Twenty20 tournament staged in England earlier that summer had gone well after that initial hiccup against Holland, and we just had a couple of games where we did not click and that ended up costing us.

I felt we were unlucky in the end in a must-win game against the West Indies because the rain did us horribly and loaded the dice in their favour, but the whole experience was a good one in front of vibrant crowds and was a great success. But what the end of that tournament meant was that the Ashes were just around the corner.

We met up as a team in Birmingham ahead of a three-day Ashes warm-up match against Warwickshire at Edgbaston, and we had a big meeting to talk about the Ashes, which really brought home how close it was and how big it all would be.

Andrew Strauss told me that facing Australia for Test cricket's ultimate prize would be like no other series I had ever or would ever play in, and I soon got to realise what he meant. The hype, the interest and the whole build-up were just phenomenal. In my mind I tried to take myself away from all that hype just to try to ensure that I remained focused on the scale of what lay ahead of us and what I needed to do.

A big help was our team bonding trip to the war graves in Belgium at the instigation, I think, of Andy Flower, which saw us get a real appreciation of the huge sacrifices that so many people made in the First World War.

I have always been really fascinated in the two world wars. When I was young I was really into history and loved watching war films, so it was something I would probably have done off my own bat at some point if I had not been given the opportunity to go there by the ECB.

It was a fantastic experience that humbled the team a lot. To see what really young boys had gone through and the conditions they had lived in was very emotional, and we went to a burial site where there were just lists of names, thousands and thousands of them, wherever you looked. I read through them all looking for my surname and suddenly there was this long list of Broads who had given their lives. And that was just at this particular burial ground. I don't think any of them were related to me, but it just brought home what it must have been like. It certainly brought our team closer together.

It caused a bit of a stir that the first Test should be in Cardiff, not least because no Test had ever been staged there before, and I must admit I was shocked when I heard about the choice of venue. To me, the first Test is always at Lord's as I have grown up with that modern tradition, and it is important to me that it should continue. But Cardiff put on a very good show. The new stadium there is not a traditional cricket ground but the atmosphere was really good and the organisation was excellent.

It felt a bit strange being in Wales at the start of an Ashes series but even that probably helped the team because if we had been in London, everybody would have been coming up to us wishing us luck and it would have been hard to get away from what was around the corner. As it was in Wales, it allowed us to really concentrate on our preparations and trying to get ourselves right, something that was to our advantage as the big day loomed.

From the moment we first saw the Cardiff wicket it seemed as if it was a flat low surface that would turn, but I do not think we expected it to be quite as slow as it turned out.

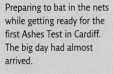

Preparing to bat in the nets while getting ready for the first Ashes Test in Cardiff. The big day had almost arrived.

We had looked at the Australian side in great detail and I had in my own mind Plan As and Bs to deal with each of their batsmen. Much was made of the lack of some of the past legends in their line-up, such as Shane Warne, Glenn McGrath, Adam Gilchrist, Matthew Hayden and Justin Langer, but we knew that in the likes of Ricky Ponting, Michael Clarke and Mike Hussey they had at least three world-class batsmen, and there were a lot of other high-quality performers too.

We knew they would be very capable of scoring runs but their bowling attack did not have quite as formidable a look about it as it did in England in 2005 and in Australia in 2006-7. Indeed, we were not too sure which direction their bowling attack would go in, but I think that it is fair to say that during the series their bowlers would often shock us with how many wickets they took.

I had done my homework. I felt that Ponting would try to pull my natural length on the slower wickets, so I had to be that little bit fuller to him. With Clarke, I'd look to swing the ball because he struggled a bit against the swinging ball in 2005, but on this occasion that was not always possible because the balls did not swing that much, particularly early on.

With Hussey, we didn't want to allow him to leave too many deliveries too early. We just wanted to make sure that we would be hitting the stumps with every ball we bowled at him, and, as it happened, he was out trying to leave the ball on three occasions in the series, so that worked well.

Phillip Hughes, their aggressive young opener, was an interesting one because he had come to county cricket earlier in the summer as an overseas player for Middlesex, a development that attracted a lot of criticism from those who feared he was being given experience of English conditions before he took on England. He averaged over a hundred during his short spell with Middlesex, but the other side of the coin was that Andrew Strauss had played with him and had a good look at him. Straussy told us that he was a very talented batsman who would be hard to keep quiet if we allowed him to get going, but then something very interesting happened.

Australia played against the England Lions at Worcester ahead of the first Test and Steve Harmison came running in on another slow wicket and really roughed Hughes up with consistently hostile short-pitched bowling. As a team, it made us realise that this was a really good way to go against him.

It hadn't really become evident that this could be a weakness in a batsman who had made a phenomenally good start to his career in county cricket, because there was no-one playing in division two who could really blast him like Harmy could.

The SWALEC Stadium in Cardiff is not a typical cricket ground but staged a dramatic first Test.

So we had spent a lot of time thinking about the Australians but we had to concentrate on our own performances. We genuinely felt we could win the Ashes. Okay, we had lost the Test series in the West Indies after losing both our captain and our coach, but the 1–0 series deficit in the Caribbean was down basically to three hours of bad cricket in Jamaica when we were dismissed for 51 in the first Test.

After that we had played some excellent cricket, scoring a good amount of hundreds, bowling dangerously and taking almost twice as many wickets in the series as the West Indies did, only to still lose.

Then the West Indies Test series in England that preceded the World Twenty20 gave us a lot of confidence because we really bullied the West Indies and scored runs on wickets that were doing a bit for Test match cricket. So we were confident and felt we had a really good chance, emphasised to us by the fact that Australia had lost at home to South Africa in their build-up for the Ashes, which was virtually unheard of in modern times. We knew there were areas within their team that we could take advantage of.

The people of Wales made a huge effort to make the first Test at Cardiff a success. That included opera singer Katherine Jenkins singing the anthems.

ABOVE LEFT: Andy Flower has been a huge influence on the England side since becoming team director ahead of the 2009 series.

ABOVE RIGHT: Andrew Strauss (*left*) has displayed a happy knack of winning tosses since becoming captain. Here Ricky Ponting (*right*) calls incorrectly in Cardiff.

The Andy Flower–Andrew Strauss axis was also impressing everybody. I had always liked and respected Andy Flower because, when I first got into the England set-up, he took it upon himself as assistant coach to try to make me a useful batsman.

There was a time during the New Zealand tour in 2008 when he would spend three hours with me in the nets during every day of a Test match when I wasn't playing in the game, and that completely changed my batting.

I had been at a stage in my game where I was consistently going back and across, losing balance and getting out lbw. But Andy changed my game to the point where I just stood there and hit the ball. We chatted about my game plan, the need to leave the ball better outside off stump and wait for the opposition to come to me, which they would to a number 8, and little things like that.

I had immediate respect for Andy because he was once the best batsman in the world, and it grew after he spent so much time with me, a bloke who wasn't even playing and hadn't at that point set the world alight with the bat. Flower is a very good technician with so much experience that he knows every batting scenario.

He also knows it is a very individual thing, and to me game plan is more important when batting than technique because you can score ugly runs in awkward ways, and that can be mightily effective.

Look at Shivnarine Chanderpaul, for instance. If you had seen him bat as a 12-year-old, you would have taken him out of the nets and tried to sort him out, but he knows his game so well that he never tries to do anything he cannot do effectively.

Andrew Strauss, meanwhile, was the captain I made my debut under in 2006 and is a very impressive character. Straussy is unflappable, keeps things simple, is very honest and very straight and will talk to you about fields. He might come up with ideas, but he gives the bowler responsibility to set the fields, and I hope he has a very long run as England captain because he deserves it and I thrive playing under him.

Our preparation was good and everyone was very excited about what was ahead of us. In fact, the atmosphere in the dressing room was unlike anything I had ever experienced before. It was very quiet, you could tell there were nerves around, and it was almost as if everyone had gone a bit internal to prepare themselves for what they had to do in the days ahead.

That is a good way of dealing with pressure to an extent, but we probably took it to extremes ahead of our date with destiny in Cardiff. Watching the first hour of the first Ashes Test was a very nervy experience and I actually ended up leaving the balcony to go inside and watch the match on the TV in the dressing room, to try to get a closer look at what the ball was doing.

We felt, batting first at Cardiff, that we needed as big a first innings score as we could possibly get to bring our spinners into the game later on, but our problem was that no-one went on to get a big hundred, and a few of our dismissals were pretty disappointing.

But Paul Collingwood and Kevin Pietersen played good innings and I had an interesting time sitting in the changing room trying to prepare myself for my first Ashes innings while enjoying the batting of Colly and KP and then the attacking strokeplay of Matt Prior and Andrew Flintoff.

Kevin, in particular, attracted criticism for the way he got out on 69 trying to sweep Nathan Hauritz, and I think he does get criticised unfairly at times. But then again, that comes with being the best batsman in the side and people both expect a lot and rely on someone like him to be a big player for us.

The way he got out this time was with a shot that is one of his bread and butter ones, but the problem here was that the bowler followed him and threw it very wide, and Kevin was unlucky to sweep the ball on to his head and get caught. I would never criticise someone for getting out to one of his regulation shots, and Kevin was as disappointed as anyone that he got out when he did rather than going on to score 150 as he could have done.

I was so tired mentally by the end of that first day because all day it was a case of 'Yes, I'm going to bat today' and then 'No I'm not, they're going well.' Finally, I got in right at the end of the first day, and the whole of that night I knew I had a huge day ahead of me, first trying to contribute as many runs as possible, and then preparing for my first deliveries in Ashes cricket.

We were a bit disappointed at the end of that first day at 336 for seven but we knew that if we could get above 400 on day two we would have a chance.

As it turned out, we had a brilliant second morning, at times scoring at more than seven an over, with Graeme Swann our biggest tail-end

Kevin Pietersen (*left*) attracted a lot of criticism for getting out by sweeping to Nathan Hauritz, but it is one of his bread and butter shots.

contributor with an unbeaten 47. At times the Australians looked rattled, and when we went out we were all geed up and ready to go. So there was no feeling that we had underachieved as we took the field to bowl at the Australians for the first time in this momentous summer.

But Australia put our innings into perspective. Whereas we had given some of our wickets away, the Australians made us work very hard to try to get them out. They left well, they played strong shots and never rushed the game. It was an exhibition of proper Test match batting and there was nowhere as bowlers we could really turn.

There was no bouncer option because the wicket was so slow, and because it was turning so slowly our two spinners, Graeme Swann and Monty Panesar, were not particularly effective either. So we ended up bowling as best we could and just hoping for mistakes.

For the first 80 overs we really tried to hit them hard, but they played fantastically well and it got to the stage, to be honest, where we just had to try to make them bat as long as possible because the longer they were batting the less time we would have to bat out for a draw.

All the way through, to be fair, it looked like a draw pitch. It didn't look as if anyone would be rolled out on it or that it would go massively up and down, so that was on our minds too towards the end of our innings when

Everything I did in 2009 was in the hope of earning an Ashes place. I made it and am seen here bowling in Cardiff.

Andrew Flintoff bowled an exceptional spell at Phil Hughes in Wales. Here he stands in contemplation (*centre*) as Australia get him away at last.

Marcus North, the only one of the Australian batsmen I had bowled at before this Test, and Brad Haddin were going well. It had become, with Australia having four century-makers, an exercise in containment, trying to make the opposition score as slowly as possible.

We were in the field for 181 overs in the end. And that is hard work. There had been so much talk in advance about how good Ricky Ponting was, and he really showed it at Cardiff. He gave no chances at all.

Michael Clarke was the only Australian I was able to dismiss, and I did not bowl particularly well, but again I did not beat myself up over that. I knew it was a flat wicket and I had very similar figures to Andrew Flintoff, to my mind the best bowler in the world, and he was struggling for ideas to get wickets too. So for me as a 23-year-old in my first Ashes Test I never expected to just turn up and get five for 30.

We were not really helped in the end by the weather, even though there had been a dreadful forecast for the Saturday in particular, the fourth day of the Test, in the build-up to the match. The trouble with weather forecasts is that however much you look at them, they always seem to be wrong. There was talk about rain and we were at the stage on that Saturday

where we could not have won the Test, so if rain had come along, it would not have been an unwelcome development.

But we are professional cricketers who want to play the game and want to see people getting play and entertainment for their money, so the only time we really wanted the weather to intervene was after Australia had eventually declared on 679 for six and we had lost two quick wickets in our second innings.

Celebrating my first Ashes wicket! Michael Clarke has been caught behind by Matt Prior.

Brad Haddin (*left*) was a thorn in our side during Australia's monumental first innings. Here he is on the way to his century.

By that point in the game the ball was zipping around under lights and we were pleased to come off, but we certainly were not hoping for rain until that late stage.

So we only had eight wickets in hand going into the last day and had much work still to do, but even though I thought about the possibility of defeat, I also knew it was still a flat pitch that should contain no demons for us.

Before that last day all the bowlers got together in a group and we had a chat, when I said: 'Look, boys, we could do a big job on this pitch. No-one can bounce us because it is too slow, they cannot push us on to the back foot. Play the line of the ball and get forward to make them get you out. Don't play any silly shots. Even if you nick it with soft hands, there's every chance the ball won't carry anyway. If we can last an hour each here, we will do our bit to save the game.'

We lost Kevin early, leaving a straight one from Ben Hilfenhaus, but I cannot do justice with words to the innings played by Paul Collingwood because it was absolutely phenomenal.

The fact he got 74 does not begin to tell you how good it was. He was there all day, basically. Colly is such a fighter in difficult circumstances, and when I got out there we just talked about doing it in ten-run segments to try to eke out the time. Again, I was saying to myself: 'Just play the line of the ball, there are no demons here.'

Mind you, we were seven down at tea, and those last two hours were unlike any I have ever experienced in cricket. I was ridiculously nervous

Paul Collingwood makes his ground during his epic match-saving second innings at Cardiff.

after getting out and not being able to do anything more to help save us the game.

Graeme Swann was batting with Colly, and they started to go quite well, so, of course, that meant that nobody could move or do anything different from what they were doing. For people who do not know, cricket dressing rooms are very strange places in these types of situation.

Superstition is bizarre. If you are doing well as a team, you cannot risk upsetting things by doing anything as outrageous as moving your seat or going to the toilet. It always applies, whichever dressing room you are in, and in England's case at the moment, Alastair Cook is the big enforcer of this particular ritual.

Cook, on this occasion, had somehow managed to get himself in the showers throwing a tennis ball against the wall, so while our batsmen were going well, he wasn't allowed to do anything other than that. Matt Prior,

ABOVE LEFT: Collingwood on the attack during his defiant show of resistance on the final day.

ABOVE RIGHT: Graeme Swann is someone I love batting with. Here he is peppered with short-pitched bowling by Siddle.

meanwhile, was sitting in his spot in the changing room throwing a tennis ball up and down, so he had to carry on doing that. And I was sitting on the balcony in my shorts and T-shirt and was definitely not allowed to go and get a jumper, even though it had got quite chilly by that stage.

I had also got myself into this routine of sitting back in my chair as the bowler was walking back to his mark and then leaning forward on to the rail, blowing into my hands as if I was a kid making owl noises.

Nathan Hauritz's selection as Australia's sole spinner attracted criticism but he had a good series.

Collingwood is dismissed by Peter Siddle, and with him, we thought, went our chances of surviving.

I know this sounds ridiculous but I did that for each ball for the last two and a half hours of the game because dressing room superstition decreed that it would be absolutely my fault if I did anything different and a wicket fell.

If anyone dared to move, they would be shouted at, and I cannot begin to explain the extent of those nerves in the changing room that day. It really brought home the huge importance of this series. You do not get nerves like that in any other contest. But this was the Ashes and it meant everything to draw that match having been under the pump for much of the time.

When Colly was out, there was a feeling of resignation among the team. It was a truly great innings, one that I have never seen matched for determination, but when he came back into the dressing room there were no congratulations or anything like that. He did not see one person when he came back into the changing room. Not one person came up to him to shake his hand or say well done. That was because none of us could move because of the silly superstitions. So Cook was still bouncing his tennis ball up the wall in the showers, Prior was still sitting there lobbing a ball up and I was sitting on the balcony, shivering and making owl noises with my hands! Colly just sat in his corner, on his own, saying: 'Cheers, lads!' No matter. He was a hero later.

When Colly was out, with 11 and a half overs to go, it left us with just one wicket left and only Monty Panesar to go and keep Jimmy Anderson company. Now Monty can look a perfectly well-organised batsman at times, though he can also miss a straight one, but on this of all days the temperaments of both of them were absolutely fantastic.

Jimmy is a much-improved batsman and showed it here, but to be honest I think the two players in the best positions were Monty and Jimmy because at least they could do something to save the match for England. The rest of us felt absolutely helpless and that was quite horrendous.

A lot was made of us sending our 12th man, Bilal Shafayat, and our stand-in physio, Steve McCaig, on to the pitch towards the end of the match, but the genuine reason was that there was absolute confusion over when the match would be officially over. We thought it was dependent on overs, but clearly time came into the equation too. So we had to keep on sending a message out, and then we would discover that we had sent out the wrong information, so another message had to go out. It was an absolute fiasco!

McCaig is an Australian, too, and was standing in for just that game for our regular physio, Kirk Russell, who was on paternity leave. He later got a verbal volley from his hero Ricky Ponting, who was not exactly pleased to

The appearance of our physio Steve McCaig (*left*) towards the end of the first Test upset his hero Ricky Ponting.

see him on the field when he was trying to get the last wicket to win the first Test.

It was something that made us laugh throughout the whole series actually. One newspaper ran a cartoon thing posing the question: 'Where's Steve McCaig?' and he kept popping up at music festivals or things like that. So in the dressing rooms we would put up pictures of him on the wall throughout the series.

Monty took it all in his stride. He can be quite an unflappable character and he just went out and tried to play forward and not do anything silly. They never really looked in any trouble to be honest, but I only really relaxed when Marcus North came on and bowled the last couple of overs. The final whistle went, so to speak, and there was never really to be a passage of play as nerve-racking as that for me throughout the rest of the series. At all the other crucial moments I was either involved or out on the field. Watching is ridiculous!

When the game was finally drawn and the crowd erupted there was a conscious decision not to celebrate too much on the balcony. It was a fantastic day and a fantastic achievement for us, but we had to remember we had only drawn and we had been outplayed for the majority of the match.

LEFT: A huge moment in us winning the Ashes. Jimmy Anderson and Monty Panesar walk off after surviving the last 11.3 overs.

BELOW: A pensive Ricky Ponting is forced to accept that his side failed by one wicket to win the first Test.

I have watched the DVD of the 2005 series in its entirety and there's a moment when the Aussies held on for a draw at Old Trafford and the camera pans round to see them going absolutely mental on the balcony. Then it goes back to Michael Vaughan and the England team in a huddle with the captain pointing up at the Australians and saying: 'Look at them. Australia do not ever celebrate a draw like that. We have got them.'

So we did not want to do anything similar to that but, believe me, when we finally got back into the changing room there were some hugs flying around.

We knew we had a lot to improve on, but we were very happy at what we had achieved, Colly, Monty and Jimmy in particular.

England v Australia (1st Test)

Cardiff 8–12 July 2009

England

*A.J. Strauss c Clarke b Johnson	30	– c Haddin b Hauritz		17
A.N. Cook c Hussey b Hilfenhaus	10	– lbw b Johnson		6
R.S. Bopara c Hughes b Johnson	35	– lbw b Hilfenhaus		1
K.P. Pietersen c Katich b Hauritz	69	– b Hilfenhaus		8
P.D. Collingwood c Haddin b Hilfenhaus	64	– c Hussey b Siddle		74
+M.J. Prior b Siddle	56	– c Clarke b Hauritz		14
A. Flintoff b Siddle	37	– c Ponting b Johnson		26
J.M. Anderson c Hussey b Hauritz	26	(10) not out		21
S.C.J. Broad b Johnson	19	(8) lbw b Hauritz		14
G.P. Swann not out	47	(9) lbw b Hilfenhaus		31
M.S. Panesar c Ponting b Hauritz	4	– not out		7
B 13, l-b 11, w 2, n-b 12	38	B 9, l-b 9, w 4, n-b 11		33

1/21 2/67 3/90 4/228   **435**
5/241 6/327 7/329 8/355 9/423 10/435

1/13 2/17 3/31 4/46 5/70   (for 9 wkts) **252**
6/127 7/159 8/221 9/233

Bowling: *First innings* – Johnson 22-2-87-3; Hilfenhaus 27-5-77-2; Siddle 27-3-121-2; Hauritz 23.5-1-95-3; Clarke 5-0-20-0; Katich 2-0-11-0. *Second innings* – Johnson 22-4-44-2; Hilfenhaus 15-3-47-3; Siddle 18-2-51-1; Hauritz 37-12-63-3; Clarke 3-0-8-0; North 7-4-14-0; Katich 3-0-7-0.

Australia

P.J. Hughes c Prior b Flintoff	36
S.M. Katich lbw b Anderson	122
*R.T. Ponting b Panesar	150
M.E.K. Hussey c Prior b Anderson	3
M.J. Clarke c Prior b Broad	83
M.J. North not out	125
+B.J. Haddin c Bopara b Collingwood	121
M.G. Johnson	
N.M. Hauritz	
B.W. Hilfenhaus	
P.M. Siddle	
B 9, l-b 14, w 4, n-b 7	34

1/60 2/299 3/325 4/331   (for 6 wkts dec) **674**
5/474 6/674

Bowling: *First innings* – Anderson 32-6-110-2; Broad 32-6-129-1; Swann 38-8-131-0; Flintoff 35-3-128-1; Panesar 35-4-115-1; Collingwood 9-0-38-1.

Umpires: Aleem Dar and B.R. Doctrove   Match drawn

5 | Second Test

Victory at Last at Lord's

The nerves had got to us a bit at Cardiff. A few of the boys admitted that when we talked openly and honestly as a team ahead of the second Test at Lord's. We all vowed to put that right at the home of cricket.

There had been no socialising with the Australian players after the first Test. It just does not happen these days. There is not really any interaction between the players during a huge series because cricket is so profession-al these days that no-one wants to give anyone on the opposition a hint of what you are thinking or what you feel their weaknesses may be. The time for that would come at the end of the series.

We drove back to London from Cardiff the morning after the game, which was also just three days before the second Test, where my first

Andrew Strauss (*centre*) was majestic at Lord's, where his innings of 161 set up our victory in the second Test.

Alastair Cook can be expansive as well as adhesive these days, as he shows during his huge opening partnership with our captain at Lord's.

assignment involved a promotion for Adidas with some of the Australian players. I headed for their Oxford Street store for the bizarre experience of standing in their window in my England kit, still as a tailor's dummy, while people took pictures of me through the glass. Then it was straight back into training ahead of the big match.

There was one bit of huge news ahead of the second Test, when Andrew Flintoff announced that he would be retiring from Test cricket at the end of the series. I cannot really say that I had an inkling of what he was going to do, but I did think ahead of the series that if we won the Ashes, Fred might call it a day then because it would be such a great way to bow out. I knew how sore his body was and how much rehabilitation after injuries he had gone through.

Every person I have ever spoken to about retirement says that you just know when your time is up and when the right time to go is, and Fred clearly knew this was the best time for him to stop playing Test cricket. He had been hurting again during that Cardiff game and I think his body was telling him enough was enough.

Fred announced to the side on the Tuesday before the game, during a huddle after the news had been broken in one of the papers that day, that this series would be his last. Whether he brought forward the announcement after it had become public I don't know.

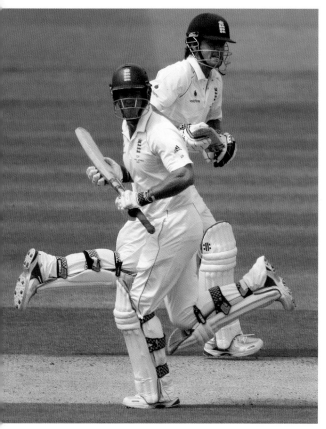

It was never going to be a distraction for the team. Maybe it was for the public, who would now turn this series into Fred's farewell tour, but for a team that is very focused on the team's goals, an individual's needs always come second.

The one thing it did do was provide yet another fantastic incentive for the team to win the Ashes, to mark Fred's retirement in the best possible way, and, if anything, our determination was enhanced as we got ready to take on Australia again.

It was extraordinary to approach the Test knowing that England had not beaten Australia at Lord's for 75 years. Yes, we all know that the Lord's pitch can be so good that it can be very hard to take 20 wickets there, but 75 years? The run had to end some time!

Graeme Swann said something really significant before the match. We had a team meeting in which the areas we needed to improve were outlined, and then at the end of it Swanny popped up and said: 'We are in an amazing position here. People dream of being in our shoes now. To play

ABOVE LEFT: Strauss (*left*) and Cook (*right*) show that they were nimble between the wickets as well as productive in their strokeplay.

ABOVE RIGHT: Nathan Hauritz dislocates his finger at Lord's, but he was soon back for Australia.

against Australia at Lord's in an Ashes Test. It is what dreams are made of, so if we do anything this week, let's make sure we enjoy the experience. We enjoy the lunches. We enjoy everything about it and I'm sure we'll play better cricket.'

It was a great way to end the team meeting. I thought: 'You're right. It's going to be phenomenal.' We were pounded a bit at Cardiff and we didn't get the chance to express ourselves as cricketers, but at Lord's we could express ourselves on the biggest stage of all.

But you can do all the talking in the world and you still need to back it up with actions, and we knew we had to hit the ground running at the start of the second Test. And that is exactly what Andrew Strauss and Alastair Cook did.

So good was our start that the pair put on 196 for the first wicket, certainly a dream start for a bowler like me playing at Lord's, who knew he could have a big Lord's lunch, the best in the game, without having to be involved in the action for a few hours afterwards!

They were fantastic. They really set the tone brilliantly and put everything we had talked about into action. The Australians were so strong and confident in Cardiff, but here they looked ruffled on the first morning and didn't really seem to have an answer to our opening pair. It looked a good Lord's wicket but they were going for boundaries all over the place and that gave us a lot of confidence.

The concentration on our balcony at Lord's shows in the faces of Kevin Pietersen, Andrew Strauss and Andrew Flintoff.

There was a feeling of 'We've got them rattled here, boys, let's hammer this home.' But after Cooky went for 95, Australia did manage to peg us back again and sadly we played a few bad shots and repeated some of the mistakes we had made in the first Test.

We finished six wickets down on the first evening for 364, but the key statistic was that our captain was unbeaten on 161, which was an amazing effort and a fantastic example of leading from the front. It meant we left the ground after the first day's play in high spirits.

I think captaincy inspires Straussy. There have been quite a few examples over the years of leadership affecting a player's form, but he really does thrive on the responsibility, and he's so well organised with his time that I do not think that the captaincy affects his training or his batting mindset.

A captain is basically an all-rounder and history tells you that it is a very hard thing to be an all-rounder at the highest level of the game. It is hard enough to master one discipline without being expert in two, mainly because it takes so much time to perfect all the elements that go towards being an all-rounder. Captaincy can really affect someone's game but Straussy has shown ever since he succeeded Kevin Pietersen that he is absolutely the right man for the job, no more so than in this first innings at Lord's.

We had obviously talked a lot about the Australian bowling and we knew that Mitchell Johnson was their absolute kingpin. He came into the Ashes with a fantastic record for Australia, and even though he has not been around for that long he was almost the experienced seamer of the side because Peter Siddle and Ben Hilfenhaus were real newcomers.

Here, though, Johnson was a bit ragged, which can easily happen when you are playing in a new country or one that you have not played much cricket in. You can struggle for rhythm as a bowler, particularly at Lord's, where the famous slope can affect a bowler if you are not used to it.

Part of the reason he struggled, though, was that our batsmen played so well against him, particularly Strauss and Cook. They made it highly difficult for him to settle, and our media added to that by running stories about his family and personal life.

Johnson was to recover really well as the series went on, but certainly that day at Lord's the pressure was on him as he came off at lunch on the first day with figures of something like none for 70 off nine overs.

From a start like that perhaps we could have gone on to a much bigger score than the 425 we ended up with, but as a Test match unit, you talk

Peter Siddle's aggression was an integral part of Australia's attack.

about getting to 400 as your minimum target and you know that anything in excess of that batting first means that you are very much in the game.

It certainly gave us something to bowl at. Lord's can be a strange ground in that when the sun is out it can be the perfect place to bat, a real bowler's graveyard, but when there is cloud cover it can be a completely different ball game. We woke up on Friday morning and it was a bit over-cast, and we were immediately given encouragement by the fact that Hilfenhaus swung it towards the end of our innings.

The Queen was introduced to both sides during the second Test, a Lord's tradition.

ABOVE: My diving catch to dismiss Simon Katich off Graham Onions seemed to be the spark to get us going at Lord's.

OPPOSITE TOP: Jimmy Anderson (*foreground*) was at his best at Lord's. When the ball swings there are few better in world cricket than Jimmy.

OPPOSITE BOTTOM: Ponting (*centre*) is controversially given out by Rudi Koertzen (*right*). We were fortunate that the contentious decisions seemed to go our way early on.

We were knocked over pretty quickly but we knew we had a sniff if we could get the ball in the right area, and Jimmy Anderson started their innings fantastically well. When Jimmy dismissed Phil Hughes and Ricky Ponting early we had a real chance in this Test, and that Friday turned into one of the most interesting Test match days I have been involved in.

There was an interesting period when Simon Katich and Mike Hussey were going well when suddenly the pitch looked as flat as anything again, but I managed to hold on to a diving catch to dismiss Katich and suddenly there was a mad period of wickets falling. My catch at fine leg off Graham Onions, who had come into the side for Monty Panesar, seemed to be a bit of a spark for us, just as Darren Gough once took a similar catch in the same area of Lord's to inspire England to a victory over the West Indies.

It also gave me a bit of confidence because I had not particularly done much in the series so far, and in my first spell at Lord's I had beaten the bat a few times but not taken any wickets. And then I took a catch that changed the momentum of the Australian innings and was a boost to me. Michael Clarke and Marcus North went soon afterwards and suddenly we were very much on top.

The floodlights were then used for the first time in a Test at Lord's and we noticed that the effect was that the ball kissed through the surface. Straussy threw me the ball and told me to try to rough the Aussies up and see where we could go. My orders in that Test were to try to hit the batsmen quite hard and I think I was timed at 94 miles per hour by the speedgun at times during that day. Jimmy was swinging it, Graham Onions was bowling a full length, and my role was to run in hard and bowl as many heavy balls and bouncers as possible.

Then I had Johnson caught on the hook and Brad Haddin tried to pull one and it looped up to square leg and I had made my first significant contribution to my first Ashes series. They were two quite big wickets late in the day and it helped put the team in a very good position at the end of play.

To bowl a side out for 215 in the first innings at Lord's was almost unheard of, and from that we had the platform to win the match and create history as the first England side to beat Australia at Lord's for 75 years.

There was one huge decision to make. That was whether to enforce the follow-on, and if the ball had swung on the third morning of the match, I am sure we would have done. Lord's can get flatter and flatter as the match goes on, so you have to strike when you can. Follow-ons would almost always be enforced not too long ago in cricket, but times have changed and wickets have got flatter, and I can understand why teams

Ravi Bopara (*below right*) came into the Ashes on the back of three successive centuries, but had an unhappy series before being left out after Headingley.

Matt Prior is a good enough batsman to bat at six, as he shows here by going on the attack.

often turn down the option of having another go at the opposition. The fol-low-on can be overrated, that's for sure, but it was a huge decision in the context of this Test because if we had not batted well in our second innings, we would have been letting Australia back into the match.

On that Saturday the sun shone and the ball did nothing, so the cap-tain decided we would have another bat and try to bat them out of the game and give us two days to bowl them out. The openers again got us off to a good start, and Matt Prior played one of the most fluent innings of the whole series.

They were vital contributions because if we had been bowled out for 200, Australia would have been chasing 400 to win the game, which at Lord's is very gettable these days. A target in excess of 500, however, is a very different matter.

In the end Australia were left with 522 to win, which put an awful lot of pressure on them. We knew as a bowling unit that not only would they have to create history but they would have to score at close to four an over to win the Test, which would have been a monumental effort.

We got a couple of early breakthroughs, which was pleasing, but by the close of the fourth day Australia were on 313 for five with Michael Clarke on 125 and Brad Haddin on 80, which actually left us a little nervous.

There was just this little nagging feeling in our minds that if they could get another hundred, they would only need 80 and suddenly it would be very close. It was almost a case of 'They couldn't do this, could they?'

But any thoughts of the worst kind of history being made against us were dispelled when Andrew Flintoff had one of the most special days of his career. He got Haddin out early on the fifth day to settle any nerves we were feeling and, on what was still a pretty good batting wicket, bowled one of the spells of his life.

Fred actually went on to only the third five-wicket haul of his Test career, which is quite extraordinary when you think about how good he has been as a Test bowler. But there's no doubt that this would have been the five-for he would have cherished most. It not only won an Ashes Test for England but it meant his name was on the famous Lord's honours board for both a century and a five-for, which not many people have done in the history of the game.

It was an extraordinary day. The whole atmosphere was electric. Lord's was sold out for the fifth day and we went ahead in the series. It could not have been better.

OPPOSITE TOP: Bowling to Ricky Ponting is always a challenge but on this occasion I was able to get him out.

OPPOSITE BOTTOM: Michael Clarke (*right*) gave us a few nervous moments with his attempt at making batting history at Lord's.

BELOW: Batting with Andrew Flintoff (*right*) after he announced he would be retiring from Test cricket. Could I replace him as our bowling all-rounder?

The image of the Ashes. Fred takes his fifth wicket on the final morning and salutes the crowd.

Personally I only bowled two or three overs but it was a privilege to be on the field to see Fred, an injured Fred at that, tearing in at them and getting the ball to talk for possibly the last time as an England Test bowler.

There were also some, shall we say, interesting celebrations from Fred after he took his wickets. We took the mickey out of him a bit for that. In St Lucia earlier that year he took a hat-trick against the West Indies in the last one-dayer, and when he took his last wicket some of us thought he went a little OTT with his celebrations, and he was teased mercilessly for it.

At Lord's some of his celebrations looked a bit preconceived, though it might just have been excitement and the hugeness of it all taking over. When Fred took his fifth wicket he went down on one knee and spread his arms out wide in what was to become one of *the* images of the series – in fact, the *Sun* urged the whole country to repeat it during future Tests!

There's no denying, though, this was Fred's day. One that nobody would begrudge him and one that propelled us to a 1–0 lead in the biggest series of them all. I think he could get away with any celebration he wanted to after that!

Lord's is a ground that Fred would have loved to have played more at and would have done if it was not for his injuries, so he deserved that very special day. It was great to see.

The match finished at lunchtime and we had the rest of the day to enjoy each other's success, knowing we would then have a little break before the third Test at Edgbaston. The Ashes had been transformed and I think the country then realised we had a great chance of beating Australia. We had not only beaten them in the second Test but had pretty much out-played them throughout the match.

Importantly for us, virtually everyone had contributed to what we had achieved up to that point. Every bowler had got useful wickets and every batsman had got some runs, so we were in a good place going into a week's rest. We had a good night out in London that night.

I have always been a big believer in enjoying victories because you work so hard for them and every Test victory is special because they are not things that are easy to earn. We have a rule in our team that, to ensure we all enjoy each other's success, we always have a drink with anyone who scores a hundred or anyone who takes a five-for, so we made sure we had a drink with Fred and went on to have a really nice time.

The moment of victory at Lord's. We are 1–0 up and have beaten Australia at the home of cricket after a gap of 75 years!

There was still a lot of hard work to do but we knew that this Australian team could be beaten. There is no victory song in the England team these days. We just chatted to each other in the changing room and Andy Flower made a very emotional speech saying how much this Test victory meant to him and how hard we had worked for it.

And I was able to get a piece of memorabilia that will hopefully stay with me for the rest of my life. I managed to get hold of one of those MCC posters advertising the game and I got it signed by all the England players. It is now framed and hanging on my wall at home, where it has a very special place.

Swanny had said at the start of the match that we should enjoy ourselves and relish the whole Lord's Test match occasion and we had certainly done that. It was a game I will never forget.

The one negative note for us was that Kevin was clearly injured and it was quickly confirmed that his Achilles needed an operation that would rule him out of the rest of the series. Everybody had seen him limping around while we were fielding, and I think the injury was beginning to affect him mentally as well as physically.

You can cope with injuries if they just affect your body, but as soon as they start hurting your mind and you start doubting whether you can carry on, that's when you have to take action. It was deflating, but injuries are inevitable in sport, and I had full faith in Ian Bell, who would come in for KP at Edgbaston, as a high-quality replacement.

Andrew Flintoff (*lower right*) walks off for the final time in a Test at Lord's, having bowled us to victory on the final day.

England v Australia (2nd Test)

Lord's 16–20 July 2009

England

*A.J. Strauss b Hilfenhaus	161	–	c Clarke b Hauritz	32
A.N. Cook lbw b Johnson	95	–	lbw b Hauritz	32
R.S. Bopara lbw b Hilfenhaus	18	–	c Katich b Hauritz	27
K.P. Pietersen c Haddin b Siddle	32	–	c Haddin b Siddle	44
P.D. Collingwood c Siddle b Clarke	16	–	c Haddin b Siddle	54
+M.J. Prior b Johnson	8	–	run out	61
A. Flintoff c Ponting b Hilfenhaus	4	–	not out	30
S.C.J. Broad b Hilfenhaus	16	–	not out	0
G.P. Swann c Ponting b Siddle	4			
J.M. Anderson c Hussey b Johnson	29			
G. Onions not out	17			
B 15, l-b 2, n-b 8	25		B 16, l-b 9, w 1, n-b 5	31
1/196 2/222 3/267 4/302	425		1/61 2/74 3/147 4/174 (for 6 wkts dec)	311
5/317 6/333 7/364 8/370 9/378 10/425			5/260 6/311	

Bowling: *First innings* – Hilfenhaus 31-12-103-4; Johnson 21.4-2-132-3; Siddle 20-1-76-2; Hauritz 8.3-1-26-0; North 16.3-2-59-0; Clarke 4-1-12-1. *Second innings* – Hilfenhaus 19-5-59-0; Johnson 17-2-68-0; Siddle 15.2-4-64-2; Hauritz 16-1-80-3; Clarke 4-0-15-0.

Australia

P.J. Hughes c Prior b Anderson	4	–	c Strauss b Flintoff	17
S.M. Katich c Broad b Onions	48	–	c Pietersen b Flintoff	6
*R.T. Ponting c Strauss b Anderson	2	–	b Broad	38
M.E.K. Hussey b Flintoff	51	–	c Collingwood b Swann	27
M.J. Clarke c Cook b Anderson	1	–	b Swann	136
M.J. North b Anderson	0	–	b Swann	6
+B.J. Haddin c Cook b Broad	28	–	c Collingwood b Flintoff	80
M.G. Johnson c Cook b Broad	4	–	b Swann	63
N.M. Hauritz c Collingwood b Onions	24	–	b Flintoff	1
P.M. Siddle c Strauss b Onions	35	–	b Flintoff	7
B.W. Hilfenhaus not out	6	–	not out	4
B 4, l-b 6, n-b 2	12		B 5, l-b 8, n-b 8	21
1/4 2/10 3/103 4/111	215		1/17 2/34 3/78 4/120	406
5/111 6/139 7/148 8/152 9/196 10/215			5/128 6/313 7/356 8/363 9/388 10/406	

Bowling: *First innings* – Anderson 21-5-55-4; Flintoff 12-4-27-1; Broad 18-1-78-2; Onions 11-1-41-3; Swann 1-0-4-0. *Second innings* – Anderson 21-4-86-0; Flintoff 27-4-92-5; Onions 9-0-50-0; Broad 16-3-49-1; Swann 28-3-87-4; Collingwood 6-1-29-0.

Umpires: B.R. Doctrove and R.E. Koertzen   England won by 115 runs

6 | Third Test

A Soggy Week at Edgbaston

We had a week's break after Lord's, and I kept remembering the advice of various players who had taken part in previous Ashes series: 'Make sure you make the most of your downtime.'

An Ashes series is different from any other, and it can be so hectic that it is difficult to unwind and get away from it. So when Paul Collingwood, who is a member of Loch Lomond golf club in Scotland, invited a few of the boys up there for a hit I jumped at the chance.

Jimmy Anderson was there, so was Ottis Gibson, our bowling coach, and I took my dad up there too, and we had three days playing this amazing golf course. The key thing during that time was that we did not have a hint of Ashes fever and what was being said back home, so we were able to completely get away from it all.

No-one talked about the series, the fact we were 1-0 with three to play, and we were just able to enjoy each other's company in the lovely weather that we were lucky enough to have up there. It was a really good idea, and Colly, having played in an Ashes series before, knew how important it was to have a distraction.

We had a really good time but there was one incident that I will not forget in a hurry, for I became the first person ever to put a golf ball through the famous old Loch Lomond pavilion, a 250-year-old building.

There is a big cark park at the front of the clubhouse and you can imagine what sort of cars you find in it. There were Aston Martins, Ferraris and Range Rovers, and that, with the pavilion behind, was the backdrop as I prepared to tee off on the par-three eighth hole.

It is about 180 yards into the wind to the hole, and a good 200 yards to the right is this car park full of lovely vehicles, with the historic old clubhouse beyond. Everyone had left their balls short, so, in my wisdom, I decided to take an extra club and really try to belt it.

But the problem was I hooked it and it flew high and wide towards the car park. I knew it had not exactly left me well placed for a birdie, but I also did not dream the ball would go anywhere near the pavilion. I certainly didn't know that my ball had crashed into the car park, narrowly avoiding a very expensive car, and had bounced up straight on to the roof of the pavilion, taking a tile off.

When I walked down to try to find my ball, one of the members came out and said: 'It's up on the roof, mate.' I started to laugh but he said: 'No, seriously. Your ball just missed my Aston Martin and ended up on the roof.' By this time there were lots of people who had walked out of the bar after hearing this loud noise, trying to find out what had happened. I think it was the most embarrassed I have ever been on a sporting field.

Luckily, it is a very relaxed club, even if it is very plush, and there was a lot of joking afterwards, with people up there saying I had been the first person to ever do that. I am pretty confident I will be the last too.

Golf is pretty big in the England team. The thing about it is that it gets you completely away from the pressures of the cricket – it gives you something else to think about, like your swing and where you're hitting the ball, so you don't think about the cricket at all.

It has been a good lesson for me. When I was younger and playing cricket I did not have the pressure of performance, of playing for England, and the media attention. Now I have that it's important to take myself away from cricket on occasion to refresh my mind and my thought processes.

BELOW LEFT: Birmingham was under water ahead of the third Test, but that didn't stop Graham Onions (*right*) singing in the rain here with me and Monty Panesar.

BELOW RIGHT: Before the third Test Andrew Strauss talked of the Aussies losing their aura without the likes of Shane Warne (*left*), who is here in his new role as a TV commentator with Sir Ian Botham.

We have some very talented golfers in our side. Andrew Strauss nearly broke the Sandy Lane course record in Barbados during our West Indies tour, and was only two shots off Sandy Lyle's best for the course. Colly plays off two, and lots of others are very capable on the golf course. This gets a bit of competition going within the squad, and when you are away for a long time on tour it can provide a very good way to spend a bit of time off from the job in hand.

I think it is fair to say that if you are good at cricket, there is a strong chance you will be good at golf too. When I was younger I remember being told that some coaches didn't like their batsmen playing golf because they feared it could affect their batting, but it tends to work that the big hitters in cricket tend to hit a big golf ball too, and the nurdlers, like Colly, seem to just plonk it on the green every time.

Colly and Straussy are undoubtedly the best golfers in our team, and I play off 18 while really enjoying getting away and having a hit.

Then it was time to look forward to the third Test at Edgbaston. We had battled with Australia at Cardiff without coming anywhere near the standards we knew we could reach, and then at Lord's we played supremely well. So we thought that as long as we could match the standards of Lord's, we would have every chance of doing extremely well in Birmingham.

The big problem with Edgbaston was the rain that had fallen for days before the game. That was a great shame because, apart from a slightly shaky start, after play eventually got under way late on the first day, we competed really well throughout the match and got ourselves in a very good position.

If it had been a full five-day Test match, I reckon we would have been in with a really good chance because, as Australia showed in 2005, you can chase big targets at Edgbaston, and we would have been confident of chasing anything that Australia left for us if we had had more time.

The first thing to say is how well the groundsman, Steve Rouse, did to get the ground ready for any sort of game after the rain he'd had to deal with in the build-up. To be honest, it was amazing we played any sort of match at all because when we arrived the outfield was just saturated and it looked as though we would do well to play any cricket before the Saturday.

Admittedly it was pretty damp and quite hard to bowl on the shortened first day because it was fairly slippery, but it was a testament to everyone involved that we ended up having as much play as we did.

The other issue to emerge before the match was our captain saying that Australia had lost their aura in this series, a statement that guaranteed a bit of interest and debate before the third Test began.

You have to remember that Straussy had played two Ashes series against Australian sides that contained some of the greatest names the game has ever seen – people like Shane Warne, Glenn McGrath, Adam Gilchrist and the rest – and now he was up against a side that contained quite a few players who had never played in an Ashes series before.

This is certainly not to suggest that the 2009 Aussie side was not competitive. We were in a real battle with them, and nobody was doubting their quality. It is just that an aura comes with being very special over a long period of time, and neither England nor Australia had really earned the right to consider that they had one. Those of us who had not played against Warne and McGrath and those other guys certainly felt the presence of the current Australian side.

The Aussies played pretty well when the game began to take their score to 126 for one at the close of the first day, but things were to change dramatically on the second.

Graham Onions set the tone fantastically with two wickets from the first two balls of the day, and then Jimmy Anderson showed what he can

Graham 'Bunny' Onions (*centre*) really announced himself on the international scene with his two-wicket burst at the start of the second day at Edgbaston.

do when the ball starts to swing. We simply blew them away, taking seven wickets in the session, a rare feat in an Ashes Test, as Australia crumbled to 263 all out.

It was a very special effort from everyone involved, particularly Anderson and Onions, and I think as a bowling unit you would take that sort of total, first innings of a Test match, every time.

Graham had started his Test career with a five-wicket haul on debut at Lord's, but that was against a West Indies side playing in conditions that did not suit them. Now he was taking the wickets of Shane Watson and Ricky Ponting, and it was really a case of him announcing himself on the international scene.

We as a team knew how good he was, but this was proof for anyone who did not know much about him that he can take the wickets of good players on good Test pitches. It was also another example of the depths of seam bowling resources at England's disposal – the stable of bowlers, as we call it – which I think will be important as time goes on and rest becomes more important for seam bowlers.

Jimmy Anderson proudly shows off the ball with which he took five Australian wickets in their first innings.

When you think that Onions and Ryan Sidebottom did not play in the final Test at the Oval, it just shows you how many good bowlers there are available to England. It is healthy because it keeps the bowlers in the side on their toes and it enables England to put out a side in every Test with an attack capable of taking 20 wickets.

Ottis Gibson is the man at the head of our 'stable'. He was a bit of a role model for me when I played with him at Leicestershire, and I think everyone enjoys working with him as England's fast-bowling coach. He is pretty simple in his approach and techniques, but that's effective in international cricket, where a lot of bowlers know their game plans already.

Freddie Flintoff, meanwhile, was pretty sore in that Test after his hero-ics at Lord's. There cannot have been many Tests in his career where he has not picked up a wicket, but this was one of them and you could see he was not able to move very well in the field. But Freddie didn't moan about that and got through it, but it became clear to us that he might be strug-gling for the fourth Test at Headingley, as it was to be back-to-back Test matches.

I struggled in that first innings too. I was delighted we had bowled them out cheaply, but I had not taken a wicket and you always have to analyse your performance in those circumstances. And the fact was, my line wasn't good enough in that first innings.

I was becoming aware that some people, either in the media or perhaps among the public, might have been questioning my place in the team, and perhaps I fell into the trap in the first innings of this match of trying to search for wickets. I would have been better off, in hindsight, settling into my role and bowling line and length to try to make sure I didn't go for more than three an over and would take wickets naturally.

I am not the sort of person to read the papers too closely or pay too much attention to the media, but you always seem to find out if someone says something critical about you. Whatever you do to ignore it, a friend will text you to say, 'Don't believe what so and so is saying about you,' and that's the first you've heard anything about it.

I had quite a few texts, really nice messages, from friends saying: 'Don't worry, I'm still backing you to be in the team whatever such and

BELOW LEFT: Our captain, Andrew Strauss, was again in the runs in Birmingham, as he showed with this pull.

BELOW RIGHT: Ben Hilfenhaus was not that well known in England before the Ashes series, but he made a big impact with his swing bowling.

such says', and a few of my old coaches were getting in touch to say: 'Don't think about changing your action'. As a result, I was becoming absolutely aware of what people were saying and thinking.

Then, when we started batting, I went out with Ottis and put a cone down on my natural length and just banged away at that cone in a practice session, forgetting about bouncers and yorkers. It was a case of hitting a length as often as I could and seeing how I went. Ottis told me to forget about trying to buy wickets and instead to settle into a rhythm whereby wickets would come naturally to me. He said: 'It's not what the ball does, it's where it does it from', and that was a good thing to say to me. He was emphasising that it is no good getting the ball to swing from three feet outside off-stump because that's useless, but if you get it to nip from off peg even an inch then you are in the game.

It actually did me the world of good. It meant that I was much more consistent in the Australian second innings, taking a couple of wickets, and that could have saved my place for the rest of the series. If I had not got Mike Hussey out straight away when I came on in that second innings and then Marcus North, I might well have been struggling to make the team for Headingley.

It was not so much finally getting a couple of wickets as the way I bowled, finding the right line and length, and having quite a few plays and misses too. To me it looked like I had turned a corner, and certainly it left me in a much more positive mood.

Up until then I had to tried to bowl in the best way for the needs of the side, something that bowlers have to do. With the team we had at Lord's, Anderson was a swing bowler, Onions a very bowl-straight nibble bowler, so the side at times wanted me to be the bang-it-in bowler we required to try to rough up the batsmen.

Some people might not understand that you occasionally have to vary your role, and, to be honest, it's normally the younger bowlers who are asked to do that because they have less experience. For instance, Jimmy is a swing bowler and you would not ask him to bowl five bouncers on the trot.

So you have to earn your right to get the strike bowler's role, and it is all still a learning experience for me as an international bowler. You have to have as many skills as possible to take wickets overseas on flat pitches. Yes, I was asked to bang it in a few times at Lord's, but I had to be good enough to hit my length straight away when I was asked to. For two and a half Tests I probably wasn't good enough to do that.

The good news at Edgbaston was that we followed up an extremely good bowling performance with an equally good batting one, with contributions all the way down the order. It did do a bit at Edgbaston that second day, so for Andrew Strauss and Ian Bell, who had come in for the injured Kevin Pietersen, to get fifties was a really good effort.

We had talked about the need for contributions from the middle and lower order, and in the third Test it was then a case of Matt Prior, Andrew Flintoff and myself trying to take the attack to the Australians to make sure we had a significant first innings advantage.

Fred batted magnificently, as he so often does at Edgbaston, and had started to get under Australian noses a bit, which you have to say is a very good thing. So there was actually a bit of heat in the middle by the time I got out there, which, again, is something I really enjoy.

Andrew Flintoff has always loved batting at Edgbaston and was back to his best in hitting the Aussies for 74.

There were a few stares and a bit of chat before Mitchell Johnson came very hard at me and Graeme Swann when he joined me at the crease after Fred's dismissal. He was right in my face after I just hit him for a four and

Exchanging words with Mitchell Johnson (*right*) in the heat of the battle. I love the competitive side of cricket.

said to me: 'Women shouldn't be allowed to play cricket. You shouldn't be playing with hair like that. Go to a hairdresser's and sort it out.'

I said: 'Whatever, mate, keep bowling.' Johnson then came round the wicket at me, so I expected a bouncer, but he pitched it up and I just put my hands through it. Luckily, it went flying through mid-on, but Johnson wasn't very happy about that and came right up to me, nose to nose, basically calling me a slogger mixed with various expletives.

As he walked away, I muttered something that did not go down particularly well with him, and poor Swanny had to endure a bouncer barrage for the next 20 minutes!

The series had started with an apparent directive from the Australian board telling their players not to sledge, but as far as I was concerned they didn't hold back on me. I seemed to ruffle a few feathers during the Cardiff Test when I brushed shoulders with Peter Siddle. I had edged him for four, and as I ran up the other end, he just sort of dropped his shoulder on me and caught me. So as I walked back past him, we brushed shoulders again and for the next 20 minutes or so I received an absolute barrage of abuse from every Australian on the pitch. Their no-sledging directive certainly didn't seem to be in place whenever I walked out to bat!

Sledging is an interesting topic. I believe there is a role for it in the game because Test cricket is a proper test, and as long as any verbal comments are not malicious, they are absolutely fine because you should be able to test people out on occasion.

A bowler has to have a presence, and if he is not allowed to say anything or stare at you, then you feel as if it is nicer to face him. I am a great fan of having a battle in the middle, and certainly in the Ashes series I had a battle straight away after reaching the middle. Whether that was my doing or the Aussies' I'm not sure, but I certainly relished it.

Maybe Australia targeted me as a young lad playing in his first Ashes series and maybe that's because they saw me as a threat. I don't know. It was pleasing to me that whenever I went out to bat people were having words with me because it was never nasty, and to me it just proved that I was playing at the very highest level of the game.

Showing that I know how to pull the ball during my half-century in the third Test.

It was an attempt to unsettle me, which is what I always expected Ashes cricket to be like, and it lived up to every expectation I had of it. I relish it. I like having my beans going. I like ticking. I think I thrive on that stimulation.

There are different techniques in sledging. For instance, I believe teams deliberately never say a word to Kevin Pietersen when he goes out to bat because I reckon he likes everyone talking to him, engaging him in banter, because it gets him into battle mode. That was the case when he went to South Africa to play his first major one-day series for England, and he was booed at every opportunity. Kevin simply responded by hitting four centuries in the series, and just seemed to relish the competitive environment he was in.

My feeling is that Kevin is one of the few players that opponents won't talk to because they just know it is not in their best interests. We have a few people who, like Kevin, relish exchanging a few words in the heat of the battle. For instance, Jimmy Anderson is very good at making the batsmen hate him, and you have to do that to be a good international bowler.

Graeme Swann calls this 'the ball of the century'. It was the one that bowled Ricky Ponting (*right*) and gave us hope of a third Test win.

In my experience, there is not really a particular side that sledges more than others. Everybody in international cricket, as far as I can see, is pretty much the same. Every team has a bit of banter and stick about them, but this is international cricket, so you have to expect that. I have never had any aggressive sledging or anything that went too far, and that's absolutely fine by me.

I tend not to say too much if anyone comes at me. I prefer just a stare, unless its exceptional circumstances, like the verbal attack by Mitchell Johnson. As a batsman, I do not think you can win at sledging because you have to get out at some stage, but the thing to do is to look in the eye of everybody who takes you on and make sure they realise that you are not going to be intimidated by anything that goes on out there.

I have ended up in the match referee's room for chat on a couple of occasions during my international career but, touch wood, I have never actually been found guilty of taking things too far. However, my dad, a referee himself, has said that he would have banned me by now if he had been in charge of any England matches!

Getting Mike Hussey caught behind by Matt Prior showed me that my bowling was returning to somewhere near its best.

I have been told to calm myself down a bit, reminded that I was on camera and told not to be perceived as being angry, which, again, is a learning experience for me. It is hard for me to think about being on TV and not showing disappointment if a decision goes against me. It is something I will have to take on board, otherwise it will start to hit me in the pocket.

There is always a fantastic atmosphere at Ashes Tests, particularly in Birmingham, and these Australian supporters played their part in the spectacle at Edgbaston.

Sometimes my competitive instinct will spread to having a go at one of my own fielders during a match, but that is something completely accepted within the team. A bowler will naturally be disappointed if something goes wrong in the field, and I am certainly not alone in the England attack in expressing that frustration.

Graeme Swann, for instance, is a big one for making his feelings known if there is a misfield or something goes wrong off his bowling, and Jimmy Anderson is the same too. Ryan Sidebottom has also been known to let off a bit of steam at a colleague.

But there are never any grudges. Nothing is ever taken into the changing room. It is very much a split second of disappointment and then you are over it.

Back to Edgbaston. Our extremely good displays with ball and bat had left us because of all the interruptions for weather, with a day and a bit to bowl them out again and go 2–0 up with two to play. We wanted to put pressure on them, and Swanny did just that with what he describes as the ball of the century, an absolute beauty, to bowl Ricky Ponting on the fourth evening of the Test.

We had Australia 88 for two going into the final day and we felt we needed to get them five down at lunch if we were going to win, but we also felt that we had a real sniff of victory. But again Michael Clarke and Marcus North batted fantastically well on a wicket that really flattened out on that final day, and produced a rearguard action that was to deny us the victory we felt we could achieve.

Straussy did not give me the ball until ten minutes before lunch on that final day, and I remember thinking that I might be in a bit of trouble and was in danger of losing my place for the Headingley Test. I wondered if the captain had lost confidence in me. But when he threw me the ball I got Mike Hussey out caught behind in my first over, and had quite a few plays and misses after that. I was unlucky not to get a few more wickets, and that day also provided me with perhaps my funniest moment of the whole series.

Cricketers always know that when things are going your way and you are in form you are more likely to be dropped if you offer a chance as a batsman or take wickets with bad balls if you are a bowler. I knew, meanwhile, that things were officially not going my way when I managed to bowl Clarke and the bails did not fall off. It was actually quite a good moment for me because I felt: 'Look, it's not with me at the moment but things are going to change now.' I then managed to get North out and the series turned around for me from there. I focused on 'Glenn McGrath'-type bowling for the rest of the series, not trying to do anything I couldn't, and concentrating on my line and length.

A lot of people expected us to win that Test on the final day but, to be fair, any team will do well to win an Ashes Test in what is basically a three-day match. There was talk about momentum having switched to Australia because they had batted out the final day, but to us it was just media talk. As far as we were concerned, no momentum had been lost and we had produced another good Test performance, having them under pressure pretty much at all times.

Within the England camp we were very positive. There was not one negative thought going through our heads as we left Birmingham and started thinking about the fourth Test at Headingley.

BELOW LEFT: Graeme Swann has established himself as the number one spinner in our side.

BELOW RIGHT: Michael Clarke (*foreground*) had a fantastic series and made sure that we could not break through and go 2–0 up in Birmingham.

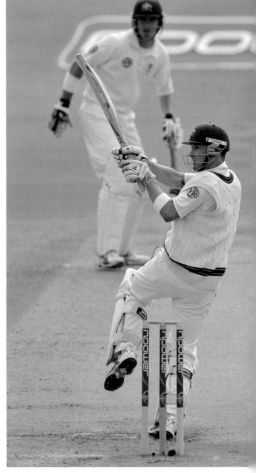

England v Australia (3rd Test)

Edgbaston 30 July–3 August 2009

Australia

S.R. Watson lbw b Onions	62	– c Prior b Anderson		53
S.M. Katich lbw b Swann	46	– c Prior b Onions		26
*R.T. Ponting c Prior b Onions	38	– b Swann		5
M.E.K. Hussey b Onions	0	– c Prior b Broad		64
M.J. Clarke lbw b Anderson	29	– not out		103
M.J. North c Prior b Anderson	12	– c Anderson b Broad		96
+G.A. Manou b Anderson	8	– not out		13
M.G. Johnson lbw b Anderson	0			
N.M. Hauritz not out	20			
P.M. Siddle c Prior b Anderson	13			
B.W. Hilfenhaus c Swann b Onions	20			
B 5, l-b 7, w 2, n-b 1	15	B 4, l-b 6, w 2, n-b 3		15
1/85 2/126 3/126 4/163	263	1/47 2/52 3/137 4/161	(for 5 wkts)	375
5/193 6/202 7/202 8/203 9/229 10/263		5/346		

Bowling: *First innings* – Anderson 24-7-80-5; Flintoff 15-2-58-0; Onions 16.4-2-58-4; Broad 13-2-51-0; Swann 2-0-4-1. *Second innings* – Anderson 21-8-47-1; Flintoff 15-0-35-0; Onions 19-3-74-1; Swann 31-4-119-1; Broad 16-2-38-2; Bopara 8.2-1-44-0; Collingwood 2-0-8-0.

England

*A.J. Strauss c Manou b Hilfenhaus	69
A.N. Cook c Manou b Siddle	0
R.S. Bopara b Hilfenhaus	23
I.R. Bell lbw b Johnson	53
P.D. Collingwood c Ponting b Hilfenhaus	13
+M.J. Prior c sub b Siddle	41
A. Flintoff c Clarke b Hauritz	74
S.C.J. Broad c & b Siddle	55
G.P. Swann c North b Johnson	24
J.M. Anderson c Manou b Hilfenhaus	1
G. Onions not out	2
b 2, l-b 4, w 6, n-b 9	21
1/2 2/60 3/141 4/159	376
5/168 6/257 7/309 8/348 9/355 10/376	

Bowling: *First innings* – Hilfenhaus 30-7-109-4; Siddle 21.3-3-89-3; Hauritz 18-2-57-1; Johnson 21-1-92-2; Watson 3-0-23-0.

Umpires: Aleem Dar and R.E. Koertzen

Match drawn

7 | Fourth Test
Chaos in Leeds

Satisfaction is probably not the right word to describe our mood after Edgbaston because as a professional sportsman you are never really satisfied, but there was a good feeling in being 1–0 up with two Tests to play in the Ashes.

We certainly left Birmingham in a positive mood, knowing that if we won at Headingley, we would win the series. The Aussies had to play all the cricket to deny us now. We had been getting wickets, and while not scoring the hundreds that we wanted, everyone was making contributions in getting us to the totals that we needed.

I had taken six wickets in three Tests, though, which was not enough, and I did fear for my place a bit. Having scored over a hundred runs and played quite expansively gave me confidence, and while I still feel I bat like a number 8 at the moment, getting half-centuries but not going on enough, I do feel I have it in me to be a proper batsman. If I am to be a Test number 7, I will have to average 40.

Reg Dickason (*left*), our Australian security adviser, is someone I trust with my life. He is useful with the boxing gloves too, as Alastair Cook discovered.

Matt Prior undergoes his fitness test after having a back spasm ahead of the Headingley Test. Thankfully, he was able to play.

My bowling was also much better in the second innings, but, with hindsight, if Andrew Flintoff had been fit for the fourth Test, I probably would not have been picked at Leeds.

I think it was quite clear that Freddie wasn't fit when we arrived at Headingley to practise. He was desperate to play but just couldn't bowl flat out in the way that he normally could. In that kind of situation you could not really play him in an Ashes Test match. It was a big loss to us, but Harmy coming back in keen to take wickets was a positive thing for the team. We lost one strike bowler but we gained another.

The Headingley Test started on the Friday after we finished at Edgbaston on the Monday, so we pretty much went straight there. I was quite focused on what I had to do and I knew I had to train well and bowl quickly in practice because of Steve Harmison's coming back into the squad.

The Headingley nets helped the seamers, which was great because it made the bowlers look good, and getting a few wickets in the nets boosted my confidence. And this was the time when the confidence and faith shown in me by Andrew Strauss, Andy Flower and the selectors was invaluable, because never at any stage after we arrived in Leeds did they suggest to me that I might be left out.

Nobody ever came up to me to say they were worried about my form, or showed any signs of concern that I had not taken enough wickets, and that was a superb boost for me.

But Headingley was carnage on the first morning of the fourth Test. I suppose we might have guessed that things were not going to go our way from the very first morning, when a fire alarm at our hotel woke us up at 4 a.m.

Bear in mind what had happened with the terrorist attacks on Mumbai and then my dad being shot at in Lahore and you can understand why I was a bit unsettled when suddenly there was this huge noise in the middle of the night and a booming voice said: 'A situation has occurred. Please leave the building.' I was like: 'What the hell is going on?' Instead of thinking that someone had set off the fire alarm, my mind was racing with all sorts of possibilities. I was wondering if someone had broken into the hotel or whether we might be trapped. I was even starting to look for somewhere in my room where I could hide.

In the end I left the room and got down to the front of the hotel, where the whole team had congregated in the freezing cold. We ended up being out there for 45 minutes and all that had happened was that someone had dried a wet T-shirt on a lamp and set it on fire.

Peter Siddle (*centre*) bowled brilliantly to take five wickets at Leeds as we crumbled to 102 all out in the fourth Test.

There were all sorts of theories about the fire alarm afterwards, one being that it was a ploy by Australian supporters to disturb us or something like that, but the truth was more prosaic than that. Nonetheless, it was pretty unsettling because the boys struggled to get back to sleep after that. It wasn't ideal on the first day of a Test, but it cannot be used as an excuse in any way for what happened next.

Freddie was unavailable because he couldn't run in properly, leaving us without both of our 'big guns', Flintoff and Kevin Pietersen, but that gave us the opportunity, we thought, to try to prove to everyone that we could thrive without them. Sadly, we were just unable to do that at all on this occasion.

I had tonsillitis from the day before the game until the last day, and ate not one bit of food for the whole match. The doctor was giving me pain-killers for my throat because I couldn't swallow, and I felt really terrible. I ended up living off maxi-muscle drinks for five days, drinking four or five a day, and lost about four kilos during the match. Then Matt Prior went down with a back spasm during the warm-up, and for a while it looked like we would be going into the Test without our first-choice wicketkeeper.

BELOW LEFT: Despite the carnage of losing in Leeds, at least I was able to take a six-wicket haul and my best Test figures. Here I am celebrating one of my wickets.

BELOW RIGHT: Steve Harmison (*left*) was back in the England side to replace his great friend Andrew Flintoff as our strike bowler. Here he chats to Andrew Strauss.

The fact that Matt felt his back during a game of football in practice drew more attention to this being a way in which we liked to warm up, but it would be unfair to blame football in this particular case because Matt was just jogging when it happened. Back problems are strange things. I remember when we played New Zealand in 2008 at Trent Bridge and Ryan Sidebottom was next in to bat. He went and lay on the physio's bed to have a quick stretch and he couldn't get off it again because his back had gone into spasm, just like that. Jimmy Anderson had to go into bat ahead of him and people were saying, 'I can't believe Sidebottom has got a nightwatchman', but he hadn't. It was just that his back had gone and he couldn't move!

Our game of football before a day's play was something that was very enjoyable and got the players going in the morning. If it was done correctly, it involved three touches and no physical contact, but unfortunately it seems as though we are not going to play football any more because of injuries that have been suffered while playing.

It is not really the game's fault. Jimmy Anderson was injured in Wellington trying to do a silly trick, Matt had a spasm while running, and then, in the one-day series against Australia that followed the Ashes, Owais Shah collided with Joe Denly when they probably both needed reminding that there was to be no contact.

So it is a shame and people could just as easily get injured in weights rooms, but I can understand why a halt has had to be called to our football games. After three injuries we just can't justify it.

That led to Paul Collingwood taking the gloves in practice in case he was needed to deputise, as he had done at Durham against the West Indies earlier that season when Matt was injured, and to talk that Bruce French, our keeping coach, might even stand in for a couple of hours while a replacement was rushed to Leeds. Alec Stewart was even mentioned as a candidate to make one of the most unlikely Test comebacks. Every name was coming out of the hat!

Nobody really knew what was going on, and the chaos led to the toss being put back ten minutes while Matt went through a fitness test, which thankfully he passed, and the problem lasted only a couple of hours for him rather than a couple of days, which was a real bonus for us.

The confusion certainly didn't help our build-up, particularly that of the captain, who was at the centre of everything trying to sort out various fitness and selection issues, and then having to think about the small matter of opening the batting for England.

Straussy only had ten minutes after the toss to get himself mentally ready to bat, and it must have affected his game plan to some extent. We'd had a meeting the day before the game and the captain emphasised to us that Headingley was a very dangerous place to drive early in your innings, and reminded us that against South Africa the previous year too many of our batsmen had got out driving.

Right at the end of it the captain said categorically, 'Boys, remember, whatever you do, don't drive early on. Let them come to you.' It was so frustrating that not just Andrew, but several of us actually got out playing the drive that day.

There is an interesting point to make here. I think if you ever tell yourself not to do something, there is an increased chance that you will do it. It is better, I feel, to keep on telling yourself what you should do rather than what you shouldn't because subconsciously that gives you a better chance of doing the right things.

We again saw too much of Michael Clarke (*right*) as he came close to adding another Ashes hundred at Headingley.

To illustrate my point, we lost too many quick wickets in that first innings and when I came in I knew I was in a battle. I was very much 'Don't drive, play in line with the ball, play with soft hands and look to clip.' Then,

last ball before lunch, I looked to turn a ball round the corner and it just looped up to the square-leg catcher.

It was a soft dismissal because I was looking to play it very softly but in the second innings I said to myself: 'I'm just going to hit the ball.' Not driving expansively, but if it was straight, I was going to see it as an opportunity to score, as the Aussies did, and that worked much better for me. It was a change of mindset and it just shows how much your mind plays on you in cricket. It is such a mental game.

Headingley, though, was to turn into a nightmare game for us. Having won the toss and batted, which I think was the right decision, we just didn't apply ourselves properly. But credit where credit is due. Australia bowled fantastically well, and Peter Siddle got five wickets by bowling a great line and length. It resulted in us being dismissed for 102, which is a terrible effort.

We still felt we had a decent chance if we could take early wickets and keep them to around 200 because the wicket was still doing something, but they came out in typical Aussie fashion and played really positively.

ABOVE LEFT: Michael Clarke gives me the stare after another competitive tussle in the middle. Graham Onions got him in the end.

ABOVE RIGHT: Marcus North played for four English counties before he made his Test debut for Australia, but quickly showed that he belonged.

We were given hope when Simon Katich was dismissed straight away, but Ricky Ponting slapped it around and we didn't bowl nearly as well as we had done in the previous two Tests. We were inconsistent.

We talked about this as a bowling unit. If you have been bowled out for 102, you are naturally going to try to bowl the opposition out for a hundred, but as soon as you try to chase wickets, you go for runs and that was perhaps the biggest lesson I learnt during the whole Ashes series.

It was not all terrible. I ended up with a six-wicket haul and my best Test bowling figures, but I was beginning to worry that there might be a

Getting six wickets at Leeds was a consolation, but it is not the same as being in a winning side.

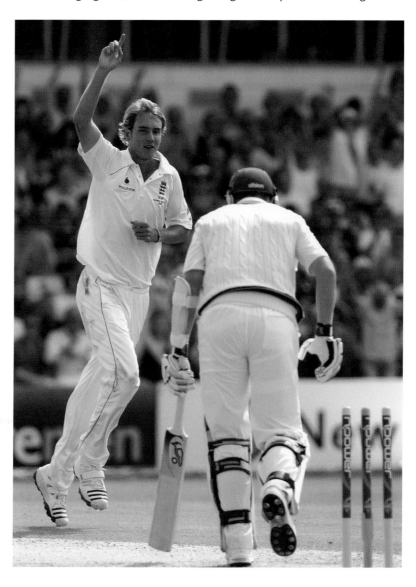

LEFT: While Peter Siddle took the wickets, Ben Hilfenhaus was again a constant threat to us at Headingley.

BELOW: Paul Collingwood trying to stem the flow of wickets in our first innings at Headingley.

curse on me because every five-for I had taken in Test cricket seemed to be coming after we had been bowled out very cheaply.

Sometimes perhaps you are just due some wickets, and I got Ponting and Mike Hussey out on the first day, both lbw in quick succession, and pretty much mopped up the tail. I was pleased, but at the end of the day it was pretty worthless in the scenario in which we found ourselves. I would much rather get wickets when it matters, so this was not a landmark I was particularly excited about. We had allowed Australia to get up to 445 and we were very much up against it.

By the close of the second day we were already five down in our second innings and heading for the most comprehensive of defeats, an emphatic turnaround in Australia's favour that had hit us really hard.

On the third morning, with the game already all but lost, Andy Flower came up to those of us who were still to bat and said: 'Boys, I've got one thing to say to you. Fight. I don't care if you go out and block every ball and

Mitchell Johnson (*left*) steadily improved as the series went on and showed why he has become such a force in the game.

stay there for five hours or smash everything, but be positive and fight whatever you do.'

That was in my mind for the rest of the day. I went into the nets and practised positively and was determined to do as much as I could to make it difficult for Australia.

We lost a wicket in the first over so I was out in the middle straight away, but Matt Prior started to get things moving with some positive shots of his own. The Aussies started to bowl quite wide to him and he was flaying them through the off side, the beginning of a spell of resistance that was to ensure we at least went down with all guns blazing.

Then Graeme Swann came in and the momentum was increased. I enjoy batting with Swanny because we seem to rub off on each other. I bat left-handed, he bats right, and we hit shots in different areas. Anything full to Swanny he absolutely smashes, while I thrive more on back of a length, and we have batted well together a few times now. This was to be the best partnership yet between us.

We again talked in the middle about the need to be positive and, while the ball was still doing a bit, we knew the wicket was flatter than at any other time in the Test. The sun had come out and we wanted to play some strong shots.

It really got going for me when Stuart Clark came on to bowl because he had come in and absolutely slogged when Australia batted, hitting me for a couple of big sixes. He had also bowled very well in our first innings, but I decided to go at him. Whatever he bowled, I was going to try to hit for four, and I took his first over for 16.

The crowd started getting going and began to cheer Clark when he went down to long leg, and Swanny came up to me and tapped bats, as we do at Nottinghamshire, rather than the England habit of punching gloves in the middle when something has gone well. So Swanny tapped my bat and said: 'Whatever you can do I can do better.'

I said: 'What do you mean?' and he replied: 'Just watch.' Next over from Clark and that disappears for 16 too, courtesy of Swanny, who came down the wicket smiling at me. I think we thrive together at the crease because we do try to have a laugh, and on this occasion there was no pressure because the game had gone, so we were just able to go out and express ourselves.

We began to smile after every shot. Swanny tried to pull Peter Siddle and ended up slapping it through mid-off before coming down to me and saying: 'That's the best shot in Test history.'

Suddenly the runs started absolutely flowing, 45 coming off just over two overs, and we noticed that the Aussies were starting to get a bit ragged. I got to 50 and raised my bat to my team-mates, and Shane Watson at short mid-wicket had a go at me. He said: 'You're celebrating like you've got a hundred, Broad, who do you think you are?' I just replied: 'You know what it's like to get a Test hundred do you? I don't think that will ever happen.'

When Swanny hit Clark for 20 in his next over Watson kept quiet and it was clear that they were getting very unhappy with what was happening. Brad Haddin was having a go at us from behind the stumps, and the Headingley crowd were enjoying it. A sell-out crowd had arrived expecting the match to be over pretty quickly, but at least we were giving them something to shout about.

We were also getting some momentum back for England, which was important because it is such a huge thing in cricket. We ended up hitting the second quickest hundred partnership in Test history and for the next week Swanny would say to me: 'How are you, partner, second quickest in history?'

BELOW LEFT: Graeme Swann (*right*) prefers tapping bats rather than punching gloves at moments like this, acknowledging my half-century.

BELOW RIGHT: Here I'm going on the attack, trying to get some momentum back from our defeat.

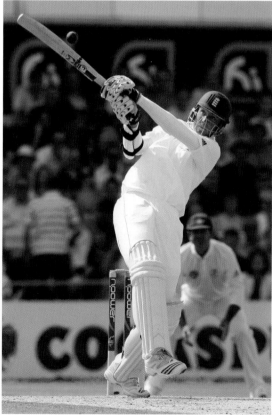

Okay, we were still devastated by the result when our fun came to an end and we were beaten by an innings, but we had had a very positive last session and things like that can change the direction of a series.

I think perhaps the knowledge that if we won at Headingley we would win the Ashes might have got to us a bit. Maybe we searched for a win rather than just playing our cricket. I don't know.

We were sitting there at the end, with the match over by lunchtime on day three, and Andy Flower said to us: 'Right, boys, meet at the team hotel at 3.30 p.m.' We thought we would just be making our way home, but instead we had a two-hour team meeting where we just talked openly and honestly about everything.

We talked about what we would do to turn things around again. We talked about what we would cut out of our game and what we would bring into it. Instead of leaving the ground on a real low, saying things like 'That was rubbish, we should have done this and that', we got everything out into the open in that meeting.

Andrew Strauss had much to contemplate after our defeat, but we thrashed everything out and left Leeds in a positive mood.

So as we left Leeds, it was more a case of 'We're going to do this, we're going to put it right.' We went away in a positive frame of mind rather than being down in the dumps. It avoided anyone thinking: 'Have the Ashes gone? Have we blown it?' And that was very clever by Andy and Straussy because it would have been easy to let us go our separate ways, moping about what had happened.

Maybe the way we batted that last day and then the team meeting that followed it turned out to be quite significant in what happened next. While the press had started to write us off, we were more determined than ever to win the Ashes. It came down to a simple equation: win at the Oval and the precious urn would be ours.

Ricky Ponting in celebratory mode with his young daughter on the outfield at Leeds. Did he think the series was won?

England v Australia (4th Test)

Headingley 7–9 August 2009

England

*A.J. Strauss c North b Siddle	3	–	lbw b Hilfenhaus		32
A.N. Cook c Clarke b Clark	30	–	c Haddin b Johnson		30
R.S. Bopara c Hussey b Hilfenhaus	1	–	lbw b Hilfenhaus		0
I.R. Bell c Haddin b Johnson	8	–	c Ponting b Johnson		3
P.D. Collingwood c Ponting b Clark	0	–	lbw b Johnson		4
+M.J. Prior not out	37	(7)	c Haddin b Hilfenhaus		22
S.C.J. Broad c Katich b Clark	3	(8)	c Watson b Siddle		61
G.P. Swann c Clark b Siddle	0	(9)	c Haddin b Johnson		62
S.J. Harmison c Haddin b Siddle	0	(10)	not out		19
J.M. Anderson c Haddin b Siddle	3	(6)	c Ponting b Hilfenhaus		4
G. Onions c Katich b Siddle	0	–	b Johnson		0
B 5, l-b 8, w 1, n-b 3	17		B 5, l-b 5, w 5, n-b 11		26
1/11 2/16 3/39 4/42	102		1/58 2/58 3/67 4/74		263
5/63 6/72 7/92 8/98 9/102 10/102			5/78 6/86 7/120 8/228 9/259 10/263		

Bowling: *First innings* – Hilfenhaus 7-0-20-1; Siddle 9.5-0-21-5; Johnson 7-0-30-1; Clark 10-4-18-3.
Second innings – Hilfenhaus 19-2-60-4; Siddle 12-2-50-1; Clark 11-1-74-0; Johnson 19.3-3-69-5.

Australia

S.R. Watson lbw b Onions	51
S.M. Katich c Bopara b Harmison	0
*R.T. Ponting lbw b Broad	78
M.E.K. Hussey lbw b Broad	10
M.J. Clarke lbw b Onions	93
M.J. North c Anderson b Broad	110
+B.J. Haddin c Bell b Harmison	14
M.G. Johnson c Bopara b Broad	27
P.M. Siddle b Broad	0
S.R. Clark b Broad	32
B.W. Hilfenhaus not out	0
B 9, l-b 14, w 4, n-b 3	30
1/14 2/133 3/140 4/151	445
5/303 6/323 7/393 8/394 9/440 10/445	

Bowling: *First innings* – Anderson 18-3-89-0; Harmison 23-4-98-2; Onions 22-5-80-2; Broad 25.1-6-91-6; Swann 16-4-64-0.

Umpires: Asad Rauf and B.F. Bowden   Australia won by an innings and 80 runs

8 | Fifth Test

Triumph at the Oval

We had a week's break before the Test that would decide the Ashes, which was actually a bit frustrating because after we had such a productive team meeting in Leeds we were keen to get on with the job in hand.

Instead we had eight days of build-up and speculation, and there was something of a media frenzy over whether Ravi Bopara would keep his place and, if not, who would come in for him. Would it be Jonathan Trott, who was part of our squad at Headingley? Would it be the prolific Mark Ramprakash? Or might it be Marcus Trescothick, even though he had retired from international cricket?

That at least seemed to take all the focus off our bad performance, which was something to be grateful for. The media, instead of nailing us for being so bad, seemed to be saying: 'We've got one Test, one chance to win the Ashes. What's our best team?'

I had a few days away, back with my mum at Oakham, and a golf day, which was another good way of getting away from the hype. It's weird, really. You would think that it is very exciting to be caught up in and be part of Ashes fever, and that you would want to be living every moment of it. But if you did that, I think you might crack up mentally because of its intensity and the expectations around it all.

I was aware that there were still some calls for me to lose my place at the Oval, even though I had taken six wickets and scored a half-century at Headingley, so it was all the more important for me to get away from everything, relax and get myself in the best frame of mind for the biggest match of my life.

I certainly agreed with the view that this was almost a one-off game and, as such, England had to go for the best team to win this particular Test. It was not a time to worry too much about the future or building for the following winter.

The calls for Trescothick were never likely to be heeded because it is well documented as to why he does not feel able to play for England any more, and that is obviously very sad because he has been a huge loss to the team.

I never actually thought Ramprakash would come in either, even though he has been such a magnificent player in county cricket in general and the Oval in particular. He had played 52 Tests and averaged 27 before they dropped him seven years ago, and I just did not think that would be the way our selectors would go.

They have big views about continuity and consistency of selection, and even though I was sure they would think of this as a one-off game, I didn't see them picking someone who might not necessarily have a role to play in the future.

Jonathan Trott was their choice and, ultimately, it was to prove a phenomenal piece of selection by all involved. It was also sensible and obvious if you think about it because he had been scoring consistent runs in all forms of the game for Warwickshire and was in prime form.

It was very sad for Ravi that he should miss the final Test, particularly as he had scored three centuries in three innings against the West Indies earlier in the year. But the Aussies had had a good run of success against him, and the pressure might have been getting to him. And you know that when cricket starts to go against you, you start to get bad decisions and some bad luck, which was exactly what was happening to Ravi.

Trotty had been in the team environment at Headingley and is a very confident fella also, and as the Oval was likely to see Test cricket at its most intense, it was no place to be for anyone who wasn't confident.

Getting ready for one of the biggest matches of our lives. Myself, Ian Bell, Andrew Flintoff and Alastair Cook take a break during training for the Oval Test.

There was still uncertainty over our final line-up as we prepared at the Oval, even though the batting issue had been resolved. First, Andrew Flintoff had not played at Leeds and everyone was wondering if he was going to be fit for what would be his final Test. And if he was fit, who would be left out? Harmison? Onions? Me? Then there was the question of whether we might consider two spinners, as we had done in Cardiff at the start of the series, with Monty Panesar in the squad as well as Graeme Swann.

There was a lot of talk within our side over what the team was going to be, and nobody knew for sure until Andrew Strauss read out the line-up on the day before the match.

I was nervous about what would happen because I knew it would be one of the biggest weeks of Test cricket ever played and I wanted to be part of it. But I had a bit more confidence about my bowling and batting after my Headingley improvement, and I prepared myself thoroughly as if I was playing. So when Straussy read out my name I was both relieved and delighted. The unlucky bowlers were Panesar and Onions, but they were to stay with us throughout the match, which was a very good thing to do. They had both made significant contributions to the series.

The next question was what was the wicket going to be like? The Oval had been gaining a reputation for draws, but we had beaten South Africa

I have always had the greatest respect for Ian Bell as a batsman, and he showed how good he was during his decisive 74 in the first innings at the Oval.

Jonathan Trott, who made such an impact on his Test debut, narrowly avoids being run out during his first innings at the highest level.

there the previous year and we were waiting to see what type of surface the groundsman would come up with.

I looked at the pitch the day before the match. To be honest, I am rubbish at reading them, but I always make sure I look at every wicket to try to have some sort of idea of what it is likely to offer. When I was younger my view was 'I've got to play on it anyway, so there's no point in looking at it', but in Test cricket there is no settling-in period during the match, so you can't afford to be unprepared. You need to know where you are going to go as soon as you start your spell.

I spoke to Alec Stewart, who knows the Oval better than most, the day before the game and he said the wicket was exactly like the ones he played on when Surrey won the championship with Saqlain Mushtaq and Martin Bicknell as two of the biggest bowling threats.

Alec told me I should bowl like Bicknell, hitting off stump, bowling straight, not searching for the nicks and trying to get lbws. If I did that, Alec told me, I would be in the game, and I left the Oval the day before the Test with a clear idea of what would be necessary to succeed on this surface.

I was pretty certain it would be a result wicket, which we were all pleased about because we had to win the game and, win or lose, at least it seemed as though we would have a chance to win the Ashes if we played well. There was no point in drawing and losing the urn.

I can honestly say there weren't more nerves than usual, even though there was such a big match ahead of us. I was lucky enough to have my girlfriend with me the day before the Test, so we went into London, had

lunch and did a bit of shopping. That was better for me than sitting in my room or chatting with the lads about cricket.

A big moment. Dismissing Shane Watson at the start of my five-wicket haul in the Australian first innings at the Oval.

It is a habit of mine to try to go out for dinner the night before each Test to try to get away from it all, and natter about anything other than the game and what is going to happen. I made sure I did that again on this occasion, but then I had a little think about what tomorrow would bring just before I went to bed.

We stayed at the Grange Hotel, near Tower Bridge, which was where England were when they won the Ashes in 2005, and it is the perfect base for an Oval Test. It is right by Tower Hill tube station, and when you leave for the ground each morning you always have people wishing you good luck and shouting: 'Come on, England.' It always starts your day off on the right note, and any hotel that has got a Japanese restaurant is for me a winner, so the Grange scores highly on that front too.

It was a massive toss to win and you have to say that, on top of every-thing else Andrew Strauss has got right as England captain, he also has a very nice habit of winning tosses, even though it is completely a question of luck.

It was crucial this time because it was clear to everybody that the team winning the toss would have the better of the batting conditions, could post 400 and be in control of the game. We were delighted, then, when Straussy duly won another one and we were batting first. The game was in our hands now.

One surprise to many on the Australian side was that they went in without their sole specialist spinner, Nathan Hauritz, but to be honest I expected that because I thought they would stick with the bowling unit that was so successful for them at Headingley. There was no-one in that team who deserved to be left out.

Although there was talk of it being a turning wicket, I don't think people expected it to turn so much from the start. There was some talk, as the game wore on, that the wicket had been doctored to suit us and was a real snotheap, but when you consider the amount of runs that were subsequently made that is quite unjust.

And then there were two wickets. We felt that Ricky Ponting might be an early lbw candidate, but here I get him playing on.

If you do the maths, it was like any other Test wicket, but the difference was that it turned on the first day as much as you would expect it to do on the third, which, as a bowler, was encouraging to see.

I was just praying we would get up to a good score, but the truth was that no-one was really sure what a good score would be on that pitch. The

batsmen came in saying that you had to hold your shape a bit longer on this pitch because it was a little two-paced. Driving was potentially dangerous because you could end up going through with it too early and chipping it up.

But after the turmoil we had had as a batting unit at Headingley I thought the way our captain and Ian Bell batted and set up our score was very special. Having said that, at the end of a first day in which we had scored 307 for eight most of the lads were a little bit down. We felt we should have got more. Matt Prior was one who felt it was at least a 400 wicket, whereas Bell perhaps read it a little better when he said: 'Boys, I think we're doing all right here.'

For all the stick Belly has had over the years for perhaps not going on to as many big scores as he could have done, he really does make good, important contributions. And his 74 at the Oval really was one, setting the platform for us.

When I went in I remember thinking I had a serious job to do to get the team in as good a place as possible, and when I resumed as one of the not-out batsmen on the second morning I felt the pitch was actually playing pretty decently.

Ponting is one of the greatest players there has ever been, and getting him at the Oval was a moment to celebrate.

The completion of the perfect five-for. Brad Haddin is bowled top of off-stump and I have the analysis that has changed my life.

Myself and Steve Harmison put on 24 for the final wicket, with Steve batting particularly well and bringing out some on-drives. And when he started doing that I thought: 'God, the wicket must have flattened out a bit.' It just seemed a bit truer and easier to hit through the line but there was still that length that kept you interested.

After we were dismissed Australia got off to a good start before rain extended the lunch break and we were able to take stock. It was a crucial time in the match and the series and we needed wickets.

Straussy came up to me before the resumption and told me I was starting off after lunch. 'Just try to get some wickets,' he said. So I went out with Ottis Gibson and had a little warm-up bowl, thinking about how I would bowl to the Australians.

Straussy has often asked me to bowl at the start of a session and it's something I have done a lot in one-day cricket. It allows you to try to set the tone but it is also a big responsibility and one that you have to get right. On this occasion Australia were close to 70 without loss and we needed to break through as soon as possible.

Simon Katich was someone, with his unorthodox technique, who I struggled against throughout the whole series and he hit me for a four and a three in my first over before I finally got the chance to bowl the final ball to Watson.

I bowled it full and straight, it hit him on the pads and I had no doubts. I was off, with my terrible habit of not appealing being noted by Billy

Andrew Flintoff has been a huge player for England and it was lovely that he should congratulate me on my five-wicket haul.

Bowden, who gave Watson out and then told me not to do that again. The one thing for sure, though, is that if you see me running off without looking at the umpire I know it's out.

So I had made a breakthrough, but in fact during my first over I didn't feel in a very good rhythm at all. At the Oval I actually prefer bowling at the other end, the Pavilion End, to the Vauxhall End, where I had been given the ball now.

The Pavilion End feels like it leads you into your run-up a bit better, whereas the Vauxhall End is a little uphill and I was struggling a bit to get my rhythm. But getting that wicket gave me the confidence to stop thinking what sort of rhythm I was in and start thinking about where the ball is going to go.

When Ponting came in it was a huge moment in the destiny of the Ashes. We all know how good he is and unless you get him early you can be in big trouble. The lads were saying: 'Come on, Broady, you can get him', and I thought straight away: 'How am I going to do it?' My plan was to try to drag him across, like I had done at Lord's, and then try to fire a quick straight one in and get him lbw.

I was dragging him across quite a bit, so then I bowled the cutter to try to nip one back and it came out horribly. As I bowled the ball I thought: 'Oh, no! I've dragged it down', but it came back at him and he chopped it on.

It was the ball I thought might be able to get him out but I had landed it on completely the wrong length and had a stroke of luck to get the biggest Australian scalp of them all.

I was trying to bowl in Glenn McGrath's style because he has always been the ultimate role model. When you consider it, it's silly to ever depart from that pattern really, because if you get it right, hitting the top of off stump off a consistent length, there's not much point in trying anything else. It is something I will have to think about as a bowler.

For this was becoming one of the best spells I have bowled in my life and all I was thinking of doing was trying to hit the top of off stump and focusing on that. Obviously I get asked to do different roles on occasions and it's good to be versatile, but there was a reason why McGrath was so successful and that was because he mastered this particular type of bowling and kept it simple.

Getting Ponting was a massive delight and gave the team a big lift too, but I could never have realised what was going to happen next. It

BELOW LEFT: The Oval crowd was just amazing during the final Test, and I will never forget the ovation I received walking off after the first innings.

BELOW RIGHT: Jonathan Trott looking calm and authoritative during his hundred in the second innings on his debut Test – an incredible performance.

Flintoff acknowledges the crowd's cheers and gets a pat on the back from his team-mates for running Ricky Ponting out at a crucial stage.

wasn't like I was thinking that I was going to run through them. All I kept thinking was 'Keep bowling straight.' The ball was swinging, but not every ball, which sounds strange, but it wasn't doing it consistently, which was actually making me more dangerous because the batsmen were not sure whether it was going to swing or not.

Swanny took responsibility for bowling at the other end and what he did fantastically well was not to give any runs away. He realised that I was in a decent rhythm and he tried to build pressure at the other end, which he did with great skill.

Hussey came next. We had talked all through the series about making him play every delivery and my first two balls I tried to swing back onto off stump, and he left them comfortably. But I tried not to panic and I bowled this ball which came back and I knew when he left it, it was dead on and I went running off again – before I realised just in time that if I didn't appeal I was going to be hit hard.

So I turned round in a desperate attempt not to get fined and ended up turning round in a circle before I ran off again. That wicket was the most exciting because we knew he could bat for a long time and it was a proper bang bang for me.

That was the moment when I thought we had got them on the rocks and I could go on a real roll. Straussy came up to me and Swanny and said: 'Look, boys, you look like you're in a nice rhythm now, don't chase it. Just bang out a length and if we get wickets, great, but if we don't just make sure they don't go anywhere.'

That was a good focus to have because we didn't try to bowl magic balls. Michael Clarke had been a real problem for us throughout the series and that morning the bowlers had talked about what we could bowl at him to be a little bit different.

And we decided to bowl just that little bit fuller to him with a drive man because he drives without moving his feet a bit early in his innings. Hopefully that would make him drive a little more tentatively, which would lead to an edge.

That was our theory and after a couple of balls he drove without any foot movement at one that swung outside off stump and he chipped it straight at Trotty. It really is lovely when a plan comes together and praise really does have to go to Ottis and the backroom staff, who had worked it out and got us to implement it.

Michael Hussey (*left*) was defiant at the Oval before becoming the final wicket in our quest to win the Ashes again.

The crowd by this time were absolutely breathtaking, something I will never forget, and every time I ran from fine leg to third man everyone was on their feet shouting and chanting.

The OCS Stand at the Oval is very high and creates a fabulous atmosphere, but while I was in the middle of this spell it wasn't something that I was really taking in. Looking back now, those moments were so special and the Oval crowd were as good as it gets. My mum and my stepdad were among them and my girlfriend's brother, who is a cricket fan and texted my girlfriend, who was at a casting for a film, each time a wicket fell.

Now it was time for Swanny to get the wickets he so richly deserved when he dismissed Marcus North and then Simon Katich, who had been hanging around stubbornly at the other end while wickets tumbled around him.

The extended session ended in the best possible way for me when I took my fifth wicket, and England's seventh in the session. And for me it was the best of the lot.

It was a dream ball for me to get a five-for. It took out Brad Haddin's off stump, the crowd erupted and I held up the ball to my mum in the crowd. I knew where she was sat and I could see she was on her feet, but at the time we were so focused on bowling Australia out that I didn't feel ecstatic or anything like that. At the time it was a question of: 'Come on, boys, we've got three more wickets to take.'

The moment I really realised we were going to knock Australia over cheaply came when Matt Prior took a great catch off Swanny to dismiss Mitchell Johnson, and one of the most phenomenal days of Test cricket I will ever experience was reaching its peak.

I went into tea having taken five for 13, wicket to wicket, and five for 37 in all. I had bowled throughout the session and I was shattered. Swanny and Fred took the last two wickets to fall and we were three down in our second innings by the close.

As I have said, we have this team rule that we all have a drink in the dressing room each time someone gets a hundred or five wickets and no-one leaves until we have done that. This time everyone was talking about what had happened that day and I didn't get back to the hotel until pretty late that night.

I was delighted to play my part in getting the team back into the game but I didn't really think too much about what it all meant until I switched my phone on again to find 75 text messages there. I was like: 'That hasn't happened before.' There were messages from old coaches and friends in Australia from the club side I played for who did so much for my career. They were saying things like: 'We're desperately sad that we're going to lose the Ashes but we're pleased it's you who has done this to us', which was a lovely gesture.

We didn't know where to run after the moment of triumph. Here Andrew Strauss (*left*) congratulates Graeme Swann.

The phone was going so much that I had to turn it off in the end, and by 8 p.m. I was so tired that I just collapsed in my room and got a film up on my hotel TV. It starred Will Smith and, typical London hotel, I paid about £25 for it before ending up falling asleep halfway through.

I would like to say I went out to celebrate, but I was more tired than I have ever been on a Test match day. There was also the feeling that the job had not yet been done because even though we had gained a big first-innings lead by bowling them out for 160 there was still a chance we would be dismissed cheaply ourselves and let them back into the match.

I knew it was by no means over so any feelings of satisfaction I had were qualified by that. I knew I had bowled well because of the amount of texts I had, but there were some tough times ahead before we could win the Ashes.

It actually sank in that I had done something significant the next morning, when I arrived at the Oval for the third day of the Test. I was asked to sign an autograph and someone presented me with the front page of that day's *Times* newspaper and there was a picture of me on it. Not the back page but the front. That doesn't happen every day.

We still had much batting to do on the Saturday before we could be confident and our hearts were in our mouths when the Australians went up for a strong caught-behind appeal off the very first ball of the third day.

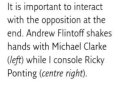

It is important to interact with the opposition at the end. Andrew Flintoff shakes hands with Michael Clarke (*left*) while I console Ricky Ponting (*centre right*).

It was a close-run thing but the umpire, Asad Rauf, made a fantastic, and correct as it proved, decision to turn it down.

The wicket had calmed down a bit and I was thinking that if we got more than 300 ahead we would be in a great position. Straussy played a fantastic captain's knock and then there was the question of his partner at the other end.

Jonathan Trott was on debut, remember, and showed an amazing temperament. But he scored a hundred in that second innings that will go down as one of the great debut centuries. It wasn't so much the hundred but the way he scored it that marked it out as something special.

It still wasn't the easiest pitch to bat on but he applied himself so professionally that it was like he was the senior pro rather than a debutant. He didn't try any outrageous shots. He just played. And that was very impressive to see.

We all knew Trotty was a good player because he had made so many good runs in county cricket but to get them the way he did was absolutely brilliant. While you were in you had to score runs because there was always the chance that the opposition would go 'bang, bang' bang' like we did in their first innings. And by playing positively we changed the momentum

The big moment... our captain Andrew Strauss lifts the famous old urn and we take our cue to celebrate at the Oval.

a little bit and emphasised to the Aussies that they would have to play very well to peg us back.

Fred played a very attacking innings to end his Test career and perhaps I was a little naïve in going in after him and trying to do the same. But I thought that was the best way to go because I wanted to follow Freddie's example. I respected the way he played in that knock. He felt that for the team it was right to play as positively as possible and as Fred writes his own scripts it seemed certain he would go on to a big one. That he didn't was a huge shame but the runs kept on coming for us.

Then Swanny, keeping Trott company, played an excellent innings to really put us out of sight of Australia. It was one of those innings when he seemed to connect with everything, and it was particularly praiseworthy because at Cardiff they had roughed him up with short balls, but he came through that and played brilliantly throughout the Ashes.

Swanny may have worn a few when they bowled short at him, but as soon as they pitched it up, which they had to do at times, he would just hit it straight back over their heads and that was wonderful to see. When Swanny raced to 63 I really thought that we were on our way to getting a very good score.

BELOW LEFT: Proudly standing with Matt Prior (*left*) and Graeme Swann (*right*), two of my biggest friends in the England team, as we are interviewed about our success.

BELOW RIGHT: Strauss displays the urn, proof that our dreams and expectations have come true in one glorious moment in south London.

Australia were set 546 to win the Test and the Ashes and they reached 80 without loss by the close of the third day, to leave us with another 'what if' situation, just like we had at Lord's.

The great friends and double Ashes winners Steve Harmison and Andrew Flintoff celebrate in the Oval dressing room.

You try not to let negative thoughts affect your mind but the wicket had got a bit lower and slower. As bowlers we just vowed to hit line and length and tried to put out of our minds any thoughts that they might create history to win this game.

We woke up on the Sunday to the clearest skies and it was baking hot too. Straussy asked me to open the bowling and I was pretty confident initially because I got one ball to spit and hit Watson on the fingers, and it was now a wicket that almost suited my variations.

The wicket had got so slow that I didn't think running in and bowling seam up was going to achieve anything. I ended up getting Watson lbw in pretty much the same way as I got him first innings and we were on our way. Swanny had got Katich the over before that and because we had gone bang, bang our spirits were lifted and our nerves were eased.

But that brought Ponting and Hussey together and they made it very tricky for us to make any further breakthroughs. Swanny continued to pose problems with big turn and the thought occurred that we might have played two spinners. With not a lot happening, the nerves were beginning to appear again.

I was in the changing room when I heard a huge cheer. I ran out and realised that Freddie had hit the stumps with a direct hit and Ponting might have been out. Everyone in the changing room was saying: 'It's close, it's close,' and then: 'Come on!' when Ponting was given out.

While I was waiting to go on to the field again, there was this little appeal against Clarke for another run-out. No-one was really celebrating but I looked around to our balcony and suddenly our people there were punching the air and shouting: 'It's out, it's out!'

So I sprinted on screaming: 'It's out!' but then followed the most horrible delay while the TV umpire deliberated, and the longer it went on, the more worried I was about the decision. I thought: 'They're not going to give it,' and the lads were giving me stick about telling them it was out. Finally the word OUT appeared on the big screen and the stadium erupted. It was, in truth, a fortuitous run-out, but it changed the whole balance of the game.

Clarke had been a thorn in our side throughout the series, but there he was, gone for a duck, and two of the biggest wickets we needed had fallen to run-outs.

Marcus North then swept but stayed out of his crease, and Matt Prior stumped him, again making me think it was our day. There was a real feeling now that we could win it that day, which would be perfect because it would be won in front of the perfect crowd on the perfect day. We were now like: 'Let's go for it.'

I was at long-off when Brad Haddin tried to smash it but hit it in the air for Straussy to run back and take a catch, and that was the moment when I thought we would win that day. We had a drink and everyone was

Ottis Gibson was a huge influence on my career at Leicester, and now, as the England bowling coach, he is integral to the success of the national team.

A special moment with my girlfriend Kacey (*left*) and my sister Gemma, our computer analyst, in the aftermath of the big moment.

high-fiving and telling each other to push for the victory that day. It would just be perfect.

Steve Harmison came on and bowled quick to take three wickets, two of them in successive balls, to leave him on a hat-trick and Australia nine down. If Harmy had recorded a hat-trick then to win the Ashes I don't think anything could have bettered that. But it didn't quite work out that way.

I was fielding at long-on when Swanny finally took Hussey's edge, the ball went safely to Alastair Cook at short leg, and we had won the Ashes. I felt like Usain Bolt. I just wanted to run to the boys as quickly as possible, and I reckon I ran the 100 metres in seven seconds, but there was no way to prove it!

I got to the huddle, where Swanny had pulled out some sort of Roy Keane celebration on his knees, and I just jumped up on top of everybody celebrating.

How can I explain what I thought at that moment? It was the best feeling of not knowing what I was feeling, if you see what I mean. It was a kind of pure ecstasy, the happiest I have ever been. It doesn't get much better than that.

There is a great picture of Alastair Cook putting the ball straight in his pocket after taking the winning catch, to make sure he kept hold of it, and Matt Prior grabbed a stump for me to keep, which I have now got at home, to celebrate my five-for. It will remain a very special part of my collection of memorabilia for ever.

England v Australia (5th Test)

The Oval 20-23 August 2009

England

*A.J. Strauss c Haddin b Hilfenhaus	55	–	c Clarke b North		75
A.N. Cook c Ponting b Siddle	10	–	c Clarke b North		9
I.R. Bell b Siddle	72	–	c Katich b Johnson		4
P.D. Collingwood c Hussey b Siddle	24	–	c Katich b Johnson		1
I.J.L. Trott run out	41	–	c North b Clark		119
+M.J. Prior c Watson b Johnson	18	–	run out (Katich)		4
A. Flintoff c Haddin b Johnson	7	–	c Siddle b North		22
S.C.J. Broad c Ponting b Hilfenhaus	37	–	c Ponting b North		29
G.P. Swann c Haddin b Siddle	18	–	c Haddin b Hilfenhaus		63
J.M. Anderson lbw b Hilfenhaus	0	–	not out		15
S.J. Harmison not out	12				
B 12, l-b 5, w 3, n-b 18	38		B 1, l-b 15, w 7, n-b 9		32
1/12 2/114 3/176 4/181	332		1/27 2/34 3/39 4/157	(for 9 wkts dec)	373
5/229 6/247 7/268 8/307 9/308 10/332			5/168 6/200 7/243 8/333 9/373		

Bowling: *First innings* – Hilfenhaus 21.5-5-71-3; Siddle 21-6-75-4; Clark 14-5-41-0; Johnson 15-0-69-2; North 14-3-33-0; Watson 5-0-26-0. *Second innings* – Hilfenhaus 11-1-58-1; Siddle 17-3-69-0; North 30-4-98-4; Johnson 17-1-60-2; Katich 5-2-9-0; Clark 12-2-43-1; Clarke 3-0-20-0.

Australia

S.R. Watson lbw b Broad	34	–	lbw b Broad		40
S.M. Katich c Cook b Swann	50	–	lbw b Swann		43
*R.T. Ponting b Broad	8	–	run out (Flintoff)		66
M.E.K. Hussey lbw b Broad	0	–	c Cook b Swann		121
M.J. Clarke c Trott b Broad	3	–	run out (Strauss)		0
M.J. North lbw b Swann	8	–	st Prior b Swann		10
+B.J. Haddin b Broad	1	–	c Strauss b Swann		34
M.G. Johnson c Prior b Swann	11	–	c Collingwood b Harmison		0
P.M. Siddle not out	26	–	c Flintoff b Harmison		10
S.R. Clark c Cook b Swann	6	–	c Cook b Harmison		0
B.W. Hilfenhaus b Flintoff	6		not out		4
B 1, l-b 5, nb 1	7		B 7, l-b 7, n-b 6		20
1/73 2/85 3/89 4/93	160		1/86 2/90 3/217 4/220		348
5/108 6/109 7/111 8/131 9/143 10/160			5/236 6/327 7/327 8/343 9/343 10/348		

Bowling: *First innings* – Anderson 9-3-29-0; Flintoff 13.5-4-35-1; Swann 14-3-38-4; Harmison 4-1- 15-0; Broad 12-1-37-5. *Second innings* – Anderson 12-2-46-0; Flintoff 11-1-42-0; Harmison 16-5- 54-3; Swann 40.2-8-120-4; Broad 22-4-71-1; Collingwood 1-0-1-0.

Umpires: Asad Rauf and B.F. Bowden   England won by 197 runs

9 | The Aftermath

The first thing we did after winning the Ashes was head to the changing room to celebrate with our support staff. I have never seen a bigger smile than the one on Ottis Gibson's face as he was delighted with the work put in by the bowlers.

We had about ten minutes before the official ceremony, time to try to reflect and let it all sink in with plenty of champagne flying around.

By the time we went back out on to the field the Aussies were already there looking quite down. They had known for half a day that they were going to lose the Ashes at some point but I don't suppose that makes it any easier when your fate is confirmed.

It was fitting that we should win on that Sunday. The crowd had been magnificent all day and we wanted to finish the job when they were all there, not on the Monday. The atmosphere would not have been quite the same had we won it at 11.30 the next morning.

As the Australians went out to be recognised at the presentations, James Avery, our media manager, came up to me and said: 'You're the man of the match', which I was surprised about to be honest because I thought Graeme Swann would get it for his eight wickets and runs in the game.

But I was absolutely delighted about that. It was my first man of the match in a Test and when I went up to receive the award the reception was fantastic and I was actually a bit emotional when I was talking to Mike Atherton.

I can't even remember what questions he asked because it is all a bit of a blur, but then we all went up one by one to get our medals and then we had to wait for Straussy to be interviewed for TV before the big moment when we would get our hands on the Ashes urn, the most famous prize in cricket.

And we had to wait for what seemed like ages as the TV interview went on and on. We had all been given a bottle of champagne and because we had taken the metal off the corks were starting to pop and fly everywhere to the point where it was actually a bit of a hazard being up on that stage!

After Atherton had asked our captain about 60 questions people began shouting: 'Hurry up, Athers', until Straussy eventually came over for the moment that you dream about from the first time you pick up a cricket ball.

What was to follow was the reward for all the hard work we had put in. As we walked round the ground with the replica urn everyone was on their feet and there was a huge flag of St George on the ground. We all lifted the urn as we made our way round the ground and Colin Gibson, the ECB's communications director, told us to be careful with the crystal glass Ashes trophy which is presented along with the urn.

We were so happy with ourselves. The family area at the Vauxhall End of the ground was particularly special. When we got there I saw my mum with my stepdad, and my grandma was there, as were my girlfriend Kacey and my agent Craig, and as I raised the urn to them my mum burst into tears, which was an unbelievable moment because I had never seen her cry before.

My sister Gemma, of course, was there too in her role as analyst to the England team. It has been great to have her around this summer and wonderful to see her being successful and being appointed as our one-day analyst after working at the academy in Loughborough. She loves sporting analysis, trying to find a weakness in an opponent, things like that, and she has worked really hard to get where she is today. Is it funny having my sister around? Not really. She has lived with me for most of her life so I think she's used to the cricket talk and the banter that goes with cricket life.

We must have been walking round the ground for about 45 minutes soaking up the atmosphere with media questions going on. It reminded me of watching FA Cup finals on TV. After the game when they interview the players they always come up with the same answers about what an atmosphere it is and how it hasn't sunk in. I've always thought: 'Come on, say something different', but then Jonathan Agnew of the BBC put a microphone in my face and I said exactly the same things Didier Drogba said when Chelsea won the FA Cup! It was the 'you've just won something special and you have to say these things' speech. I'm not sure there really is anything else to say at those moments.

We all then sat down on the pitch, took our boots off after a long day and had a beer together on the pitch, then all the families joined us in the changing room while the sun was still setting for about an hour and a half for plenty of champagne.

My grandma, who was about to celebrate her 80th birthday, was as happy as I've ever seen her and seemed to give everyone a kiss as they walked up the stairs. She had never met any of them in her life and people must have been thinking: 'Who's this old dear giving everyone a kiss?'

Once the families moved back to the hotel the Aussies came in for a drink for another hour and a half. I spoke to Shane Watson, Nathan Hauritz and Marcus North and you do really get a different perspective on people you have played against when you meet them properly off the pitch.

Matt Prior, myself and Jimmy Anderson went to get a beer out in the big baths at the back of the changing room and ended up chatting and it was lovely just nattering away in a corner. Steve Harmison then came in and we realised it was the moment we should start to enjoy our success as a team with nobody else there.

The Aussies were fantastic. They wished us well before Ricky Ponting said: 'Look lads, enjoy your success, we're going to shoot off.'

After a while we realised we should go back to the hotel and we were taken across town back to the City Grange, with paparazzi following us and the boys getting giddy on champagne and shouting out of the windows.

A lovely function was put on for us at the hotel in one of the suites upstairs and I was still in my whites with two medals around my neck. And that's how I woke up the next day at around 8 a.m.

In 2005 there was an open-top bus celebration and MBEs all round but that happened because we had not won the Ashes for 20 years so that was understandable. The schedule was very different this time and we were shooting straight off to Ireland for a one-day international so there wasn't time for a bus or to meet the prime minister, anything like that.

Maybe it was a little more low-key but not in the players' eyes. We enjoyed our success and it really was the best moment a cricketer could have. We had to move on quickly but it was important not to forget how much this meant because it is what we work for and dream about.

Since the game people have told me that I produced one of the great spells of Ashes bowling, but I'm still not very conscious of that. To me I got a few wickets in a spell where the ball came out quite nicely, and more importantly we got pressure on them as a team and bowled them out. But I think as time goes on people remember these things more. At the moment it is still fresh in my mind.

As a team it is very important we do not consider the Ashes the be-all and end-all. Our goal is to become the best team in the world, so beating Australia at home is a stepping stone along the way. It is important to celebrate your success along with the public and then get stronger for the experience.

Life has changed a little bit for me since then. I was called 'Golden Bowls' for instance by one paper! The day after we won the Ashes I gave a press conference where I was asked about paparazzi and David Beckham and sponsorship deals.

But I am very lucky in that I have got some very good people around me and I have made my one and only goal to play my part in making England the best side in the world. And I can only do that by taking wickets and scoring runs.

The people around me look after everything else. My mum takes the stresses and strains of life off me by looking after my finances and things like that. If there is a gas bill sitting at home for me while I'm away playing cricket, she will look after it rather than having me come home to find myself cut off.

My agent is not a typical agent. Craig Sackfield is more of a friend who looks after me as a person rather than as a sportsman to cash in on. He has clear ideas of where he wants me to go and we think along the same lines.

I want to be thought of as a cricketer and remembered for what I did on the pitch rather than for any off-field stuff, and I am as determined as ever for that to happen.

Being invited on to the Jonathan Ross TV show was different, though. That was a special occasion for me, mainly because Ricky Gervais, a fellow guest, is one of my heroes and I've got a picture of him on my wall at home as David Brent in *The Office*.

As I had a team meeting beforehand, I was running late and didn't meet Jonathan until I went out on stage. I was a bit nervous but he was fantastic and made me feel welcome. Then I got to bowl at them all in the nets for the show, and Ricky said it was the most scared he had been since he was 13, when the big guys were always bouncing him in the nets. It took him back to his schooldays!

Jamie Oliver, another guest, had the best technique. His mum and dad own a pub called the Cricketers and he said he has spent a lot of time around cricket. But he also said that the other players laughed at him as a kid because at the time he was into *Star Wars* rather than cricket and used to see a cricket box as something to put on your face so you could talk like Darth Vader. He didn't know why people were laughing at him!

I remember, when I was in my teens, reading about a sportsman who had got to be number 1 in the world very quickly before falling down very quickly. They said that because they had reached their ultimate goal so young they didn't reset their goals. Now I want to make sure that winning the Ashes at home was just one of my goals and I keep setting new ones.

We are on a journey, and as I speak, beating South Africa in South Africa is a huge goal, as is retaining the Ashes in Australia next winter. It is very rare that the Aussies lose at home to anyone, so that has to be a major aim for us. It is a realistic one.

Andy Flower is huge on the concept of constant improvement. It's one of his bullet points. To become an England player and stay one you have to keep getting better, and it has been good for the team to realise that there are bigger things out there to achieve.

I have joined my dad in becoming an Ashes winner at 23 years of age, but I sincerely hope the best is yet to come.

PART 3

The Players

Andrew Strauss

Born: 2 March 1977
Batting style: Left-handed
Bowling style: Left-arm medium

2009 Ashes Record

Matches	Innings	Not out	Runs	Highest score	Average	100s	50s
5	9	0	474	161	52.66	1	3

Test Career Record (2004-9)

Matches	Innings	Not out	Runs	Highest score	Average	100s	50s
67	123	5	5266	177	44.62	18	17

I've already been fortunate enough to play under some very good England captains in my short time as a player. Michael Vaughan taught me a huge amount, and Straussy is similar in that he remains calm, authoritative and unfazed under pressure.

I really am thriving under Straussy. He is assertive and strong in his views but he will listen to a bowler and what fields he wants and plans he wants to execute. If you go for a couple of fours, he will come up and say: 'What do you think?' rather than: 'Come on, sort it out', and that's a huge strength of his. I believe he could be England captain for a very long time and become a very successful one.

PREVIOUS PAGES: Graeme Swann takes the last Australian wicket, Mike Hussey caught and pocketed by Alastair Cook, and the Ashes are won.

Jimmy Anderson

Born: 30 July 1982
Batting style: Left-handed
Bowling style: Right-arm fast-medium

2009 Ashes Record

Matches	Innings	Not out	Runs	Highest score	Average	100s	50s	
5	8	2	99	29	16.50	0	0	

Matches	Overs	Runs	Wickets	Average	Runs per over	Best bowling	5 in an innings	10 in a match
5	158	542	12	45.16	3.43	5-80	1	0

Test Career Record (2003-9)

Matches	Innings	Not out	Runs	Highest score	Average	100s	50s	
42	56	27	412	34	14.20	0	0	

Matches	Overs	Runs	Wickets	Average	Runs per over	Best bowling	5 in an innings	10 in a match
42	1408.5	4883	140	34.87	3.46	7-43	7	0

Jimmy is one of the best swing bowlers in the world and a great bloke to have around. I think he and Swanny want to have their own comedy TV show when they are done. We call them Tweedledee and Tweedledum, but I think they prefer to think of themselves as Morecambe and Wise!

Swanny is very outgoing in public, but Jimmy can be shy with the media, so perhaps people don't realise what he is really like. He's a real character in the dressing room and a great help to me as a bowler. He's played a lot of cricket and has gone through huge ups and downs, so to have him around is superb.

Jimmy has become much more consistent over the last couple of years and can swing the ball both in and out and lands them on a good length more often that not. Picked up some crucial wickets throughout the series and was at his absolute best at Edgbaston and at times at Lord's. I think he will go on to become one of the great England bowlers.

Ian Bell

Born: 11 April 1982
Batting style: Right-handed
Bowling style: Right-arm medium

2009 Ashes Record

Matches	Innings	Not out	Runs	Highest score	Average	100s	50s
3	5	0	140	72	28.00	0	2

Test Career Record (2004–9)

Matches	Innings	Not out	Runs	Highest score	Average	100s	50s
49	88	9	3144	199	39.79	8	21

Matches	Overs	Runs	Wickets	Average	Runs per over	Best bowling	5 in an innings	10 in a match
49	18	76	1	76.00	4.22	1-33	0	0

Has had a tough time since January, when he was left out of our side after the first Test in Jamaica against the West Indies, but I have always considered him one of the most technically gifted batsmen in the country.

He couldn't have been tested more temperamentally by being brought into the middle of an Ashes series having been dropped earlier in the year, and to get a half-century on his home ground at Edgbaston coming back into the side was very special for him. Stood up in other crucial moments too, and I do believe his 74 on the first day of the final Test at the Oval got us out of a hole and will give Belly a huge amount of confidence to establish himself further as a batsman of the highest quality.

Ravi Bopara

Born: 4 May 1985
Batting style: **Right-handed**
Bowling style: **Right-arm medium**

2009 Ashes Record

Matches	Innings	Not out	Runs	Highest score	Average	100s	50s	
4	7	0	105	35	15.00	0	0	

Matches	Overs	Runs	Wickets	Average	Runs per over	Best bowling	5 in an innings	10 in a match
4	8.2	44	0	–	5.28	–	0	0

Test Career Record (2007–9)

Matches	Innings	Not out	Runs	Highest score	Average	100s	50s	
10	15	0	502	143	33.45	3	0	

Matches	Overs	Runs	Wickets	Average	Runs per over	Best bowling	5 in an innings	10 in a match
10	49.2	199	1	199.00	4.03	1–39	0	0

It was a huge shame that Ravi wasn't on the podium with us to celebrate our Ashes success. It was noticed by the players too, who were saying: 'Where's Ravi?' and were very disappointed that he had to play a game elsewhere for Essex. Ravi had a tough series and was given a hard time by the Aussies, but he was in four out of the five Tests and played his part.

Ravi is a hugely talented player who has bounced back from Test disappointment before and will do so again. I was disappointed that he didn't score more runs in the Ashes after hitting three centuries in consecutive innings against the West Indies earlier that year, but I know he will be back and I confidently predict he will average more than 40 in Test cricket before his time is up. Whether number 5 is a better batting place for him than 3 remains to be seen.

Stuart Broad

Born: 24 June 1986
Batting style: Left-handed
Bowling style: Right-arm fast-medium

2009 Ashes Record

Matches	Innings	Not out	Runs	Highest score	Average	100s	50s	
5	9	1	234	61	29.25	0	2	

Matches	Overs	Runs	Wickets	Average	Runs per over	Best bowling	5 in an innings	10 in a match
5	154.1	544	18	30.22	3.52	6-91	2	0

Test Career Record (2007–9)

Matches	Innings	Not out	Runs	Highest score	Average	100s	50s	
22	31	6	767	76	30.68	0	5	

Matches	Overs	Runs	Wickets	Average	Runs per over	Best bowling	5 in an innings	10 in a match
22	697.5	2290	64	35.78	3.28	6-91	3	0

I am delighted and privileged to have played three years of international cricket now all around the world. The last day at the Oval is one I will never forget, but the journey must start there rather than be seen by me or any-one else as some sort of peak.

'Always reset your goals,' Andy Flower says, and for me, as I write, that now means the tour of South Africa and next year's Ashes in Australia. If we can win there and I am in the team, then I really will be a very satisfied cricketer.

Paul Collingwood

Born: 26 May 1976
Batting style: Right-handed
Bowling style: Right-arm medium

2009 Ashes Record

Matches	Innings	Not out	Runs	Highest score	Average	100s	50s	
5	9	0	250	74	27.77	0	3	

Matches	Overs	Runs	Wickets	Average	Runs per over	Best bowling	5 in an innings	10 in a match
5	18	76	1	76.00	4.22	1-38	0	0

Test Career Record (2003–9)

Matches	Innings	Not out	Runs	Highest score	Average	100s	50s	
53	93	9	3565	206	42.44	9	16	

Matches	Overs	Runs	Wickets	Average	Runs per over	Best bowling	5 in an innings	10 in a match
53	254.3	846	15	56.40	3.32	3-23	0	0

Colly's stand-out performance in the Ashes was that innings of pure defiance at Cardiff, which did so much to ensure we were still on level terms going to Lord's. You will struggle to find anyone else in the country with the mental strength to play an innings like that. He's a fantastic man to have in the changing room and is so experienced that he can deal with any situation. He is a more than useful bowler, an excellent fielder and has now added a new skill: he has taken on Marcus Trescothick's old mantle as the team's official ball-shiner. He really gives the ball a shine and takes good care to make sure it is ready when we want to try reverse-swinging it.

Another one who didn't get the runs he would have liked, but he played some crucial knocks and was typical of our ability to seize the big moments in the series.

Alastair Cook

Born: 25 December 1984
Batting style: Left-handed
Bowling style: Right off-break

2009 Ashes Record

Matches	Innings	Not out	Runs	Highest score	Average	100s	50s
5	9	0	222	95	24.66	0	1

Test Career Record (2006–9)

Matches	Innings	Not out	Runs	Highest score	Average	100s	50s
48	87	5	3509	160	42.79	9	20

Matches	Overs	Runs	Wickets	Average	Runs per over	Best bowling	5 in an innings	10 in a match
48	1	1	0	–	1	–	0	0

One of the most consistent young batsmen in the world. He just seems to bang out runs again and again. He averages in the forties and has nine Test hundreds already at the age of 24, a record that stands comparison with the greats of the game.

He is also a very calm character, which bodes well for the future, because I do see him as a future England captain. He doesn't give too much away but is relaxed in the dressing room, which is what you need. Cooky probably didn't get the runs he would have wanted to in the Ashes series but he will soon put that behind him. He is going to be a phenomenal Test cricketer for the next ten years. The classic old head on young shoulders.

Andrew Flintoff

Born: **6 December 1977**
Batting style: **Right-handed**
Bowling style: **Right-arm fast**

2009 Ashes Record

Matches	Innings	Not out	Runs	Highest score	Average	100s	50s		
4	7	1	200	74	33.33	0	1		

Matches	Overs	Runs	Wickets	Average	Runs per over	Best bowling	5 in an innings	10 in a match
4	128.5	417	8	52.12	3.23	5-92	1	0

Test Career Record (1998–2009)

Matches	Innings	Not out	Runs	Highest score	Average	100s	50s		
79	130	9	3845	167	31.77	5	26		

Matches	Overs	Runs	Wickets	Average	Runs per over	Best bowling	5 in an innings	10 in a match
79	2491.5	7410	226	32.78	2.97	5-58	3	0

I have been privileged to play Test cricket with Fred. He is a character I admired when I was growing up and he keeps his game very simple, which is a good example to any young player coming through in the game. When he bowls all he focuses on is hitting the top of off stump, and when he bats he just tries to hit the ball as hard as he can. Okay, he had fitness issues throughout the Ashes and didn't have the series he had in 2005, but his spell at Lord's which won the second Test was as good as any spell you will ever see on what was still a flat wicket.

The crowd love seeing Fred succeed, and one of the best moments of the summer for me was seeing his name go up on the Lord's honours board for a five-wicket haul as well as a Test century in 2004. It is very special to get up there for both bowling and batting, and very few people have done that. Fred has managed to achieve something that I dream about achieving too.

Steve Harmison

Born: 23 October 1978
Batting style: Right-handed
Bowling style: Right-arm fast

2009 Ashes Record

Matches	Innings	Not out	Runs	Highest score	Average	100s	50s		
2	3	2	31	19 not out	31.00	0	0		

Matches	Overs	Runs	Wickets	Average	Runs per over	Best bowling	5 in an innings	10 in a match
2	43	167	5	33.40	3.88	3-54	0	0

Test Career Record (2002-9)

Matches	Innings	Not out	Runs	Highest score	Average	100s	50s		
63	89	23	743	49 not out	11.79	0	0		

Matches	Overs	Runs	Wickets	Average	Runs per over	Best bowling	5 in an innings	10 in a match
63	2229.1	7192	226	31.82	3.22	7-12	8	1

Harmy came in for the last two Tests, and I don't think there would have been a more fitting way to win the Ashes than for him to get a hat-trick in that last game. I think he could have just walked off into the sunset with the perfect way of going out if he had achieved that! When Steve is fit and firing he's one of the most dangerous bowlers in the country, and to have him at the Oval, where we knew it would bounce and taller bowlers would be effective, was excellent.

Harmy has his critics but one thing that people do not always see is that he is very supportive of his team-mates. When I had a couple of average Tests at Cardiff and Lord's he was one of the first to put his arm round me and say: 'Just focus on what you do best. Don't worry about that.' His advice was excellent and shows the consideration he has for others when he is fighting for a place himself.

Graham Onions

Born: **9 September 1982**
Batting style: **Right-handed**
Bowling style: **Right-arm medium-fast**

2009 Ashes Record

Matches	Innings	Not out	Runs	Highest score	Average	100s	50s		
3	4	2	19	17 not out	9.50	0	0		

Matches	Overs	Runs	Wickets	Average	Runs per over	Best bowling	5 in an innings	10 in a match
3	77.4	303	10	30.30	3.90	4-58	0	0

Test Career Record (2009–9)

Matches	Innings	Not out	Runs	Highest score	Average	100s	50s		
5	5	2	19	17 not out	6.33	0	0		

Matches	Overs	Runs	Wickets	Average	Runs per over	Best bowling	5 in an innings	10 in a match
5	123.1	503	20	25.15	4.08	7-102	1	0

'Bunny', as we call him, to me played a big part in the Ashes success even though he was unlucky to miss out on the final Test at the Oval. He showed what a quality bowler he is by taking more than 80 wickets in the 2009 season with the method of bowling straight, hitting the deck and nibbling it, which is always a dangerous combination.

I shared a room with Graham on my first academy tour for six weeks and he is a really lovely fella who I have been delighted to see come in and do so well. Deserves the award of a central contract that came his way at the end of the 2009 season. Got a great future ahead of him.

Monty Panesar

Born: 25 April 1982
Batting style: Left-handed
Bowling style: Left-arm slow orthodox

2009 Ashes Record

Matches	Innings	Not out	Runs	Highest score	Average	100s	50s		
1	2	1	11	7 not out	11.00	0	0		

Matches	Overs	Runs	Wickets	Average	Runs per over	Best bowling	5 in an innings	10 in a match
1	35	115	1	115.00	3.28	1-115	0	0

Test Career Record (2006–9)

Matches	Innings	Not out	Runs	Highest score	Average	100s	50s		
39	51	17	187	26	5.50	0	0		

Matches	Overs	Runs	Wickets	Average	Runs per over	Best bowling	5 in an innings	10 in a match
39	1507	4331	126	34.37	2.87	6-37	8	1

Monty was the reason why we were all absolute nervous wrecks in those dramatic closing stages at Cardiff, because deep in our hearts I am not sure any of us expected him to survive 11 overs and 3 balls and hold on for a draw with Jimmy. Anyone who has seen Monty in the nets will know why we felt that way, but he showed fantastic temperament with the bat and hopefully that will give him confidence to get his Test career back on track.

Had a fantastic start to life with England, but has now experienced tougher times and it will be up to him to take more wickets to get himself back in the reckoning. I'm sure he will because he is a very talented spin bowler and a very likeable man. People want to see him back with England, and I'm sure they will get their wish.

Kevin Pietersen

Born: 27 June 1980
Batting style: Right-handed
Bowling style: Right-arm off-break

2009 Ashes Record

Matches	Innings	Not out	Runs	Highest score	Average	100s	50s
2	4	0	153	69	38.25	0	1

Test Career Record (2005-9)

Matches	Innings	Not out	Runs	Highest score	Average	100s	50s
54	97	4	4647	226	49.96	16	15

Matches	Overs	Runs	Wickets	Average	Runs per over	Best bowling	5 in an innings	10 in a match
54	122.3	518	4	129.50	4.22	1-0	0	0

Everyone knows what he is capable of, and Kevin was a huge loss when he had to concede defeat and have an operation on his Achilles after the Lord's Test. But he remained incredibly supportive to us throughout the series. He's the sort of tough character you always want on your side and he enjoyed the competitive side of the game. The team were delighted to have won the Ashes without him because it means when he comes back we will be an even stronger side and we can go a lot further in the game.

Started the series with a good contribution at Cardiff although his injury was hampering him even then, and we all know that when he gets fully fit he will be a run machine again for many years to come.

Matt Prior

Born: 26 February 1982
Batting style: Right-handed
Wicketkeeper

2009 Ashes Record

Matches	Innings	Not out	Runs	Highest score	Average	100s	50s
5	9	1	261	61	32.62	0	2

Test Career Record (2007–09)

Matches	Innings	Not out	Runs	Highest score	Average	100s	50s
23	37	7	1326	131 not out	44.20	2	10

Matt is one of the unsung heroes of our Ashes success because his flamboyant batting sets up the tail to really kick on and get as many runs as possible all the way down. At number 6 he gives the side a huge amount of balance, which no keeper-batsman has really done in the England team since Alec Stewart. Prior's strokeplay excites the crowd, and he made some crucial contributions throughout the series.

The thing that will please him and everyone the most is that throughout the whole series no-one whispered anything about his glovework. His keeping was immaculate and he got his just rewards when he took that fantastic sharp stumping of Marcus North on the last day of the series. I think Matt has a long England career ahead of him.

Graeme Swann

Born: 24 March 1979
Batting style: Right-handed
Bowling style: Right-arm off-break

2009 Ashes Record

Matches	Innings	Not out	Runs	Highest score	Average	100s	50s
5	8	1	249	63	35.57	0	2

Matches	Overs	Runs	Wickets	Average	Runs per over	Best bowling	5 in an innings	10 in a match
5	170.2	567	14	40.50	3.32	4-38	0	0

Test Career Record (2008-9)

Matches	Innings	Not out	Runs	Highest score	Average	100s	50s
12	14	4	354	63 not out	35.4	0	3

Matches	Overs	Runs	Wickets	Average	Runs per over	Best bowling	5 in an innings	10 in a match
12	490.1	1459	48	30.39	2.97	5-57	2	0

My Nottinghamshire team-mate and the joker of the pack. Swanny keeps everyone entertained even when we're doing badly, which is crucial because every side needs someone like that. If there were two Swannys it would get a bit over the top, but one is perfect! He had a fantastic series as our number one spinner, particularly at the Oval, where he got eight wickets and deserved the man of the match award. But it was his batting that thrilled me the most. The ball he bowled to dismiss Ricky Ponting at Edgbaston has been classed as the ball of the century – by Swanny! I'm not sure anyone else is saying that, but Swanny is shouting it from the rooftops.

I love batting with him and will always remember our 100 partnership off 73 balls at Headingley, even if it was in a losing cause. We just had such good fun, and it proved that when you do have good fun you can play good cricket. Adds great balance to the side too as an off-spinner who makes huge contributions at number 9. Had to work very hard for his chance and I'm delighted he's now in the top ten in the world because he deserves to be there.

Jonathan Trott

Born: 22 April 1981
Batting style: Right-handed
Bowling style: Right-arm medium

2009 Ashes Record

Matches	Innings	Not out	Runs	Highest score	Average	100s	50s
1	2	0	160	119	80.00	1	0

Could quite easily be classed as having had the best debut of all time in Test cricket by an England player. To come in under such pressure and to play with such composure was impressive. Looks like a very solid player to have at number 5 in your line-up and looks set to have a really good international career because he knows his game plan and is coming in at an age when he can thrive straight away.

Ricky Ponting

Born: 19 December 1974
Batting style: Right-handed
Bowling style: Right-arm fast-medium; right-arm off-break

2009 Ashes Record

Matches	Innings	Not out	Runs	Highest score	Average	100s	50s
5	8	0	385	150	48.12	1	2

Test Career Record (1995–2009)

Matches	Innings	Not out	Runs	Highest score	Average	100s	50s
136	229	26	11345	257	55.88	38	48

Matches	Overs	Runs	Wickets	Average	Runs per over	Best bowling	5 in an innings	10 in a match
136	89.5	242	5	48.40	2.69	1–0	0	0

A player I have admired for years, and to come up against him and have a battle with him was fantastic. Ponting is the sort of batsman who pulls my natural length, so I had to adjust and look to go a little bit fuller to him. To dismiss him three times in the series was highly satisfying for me, because not only is he one of the all-time great batsmen, but he also gives you nothing on the pitch. He didn't really acknowledge us as players and didn't say a word to me for the whole series, but I've heard he's a nice bloke off the pitch. I have respect for his attitude because he was here to win rather than be nice, and I'm sure he will make it his career goal now to come back to England in 2013 and win the Ashes again after losing them twice here as skipper.

Stuart Clark

Born: 28 September 1975
Batting style: Right-handed
Bowling style: Right-arm fast-medium

2009 Ashes Record

Matches	Innings	Not out	Runs	Highest score	Average	100s	50s	
2	3	0	38	32	12.66	0	0	

Matches	Overs	Runs	Wickets	Average	Runs per over	Best bowling	5 in an innings	10 in a match
2	47	176	4	44.00	3.74	3-18	0	2

Frustrated me at Headingley by slogging me for two big sixes, but I suppose he had a licence to. So Swanny and I made it our game plan to try to hit him out of their attack, which worked for a while.

Clark was the man who bowled us out in Australia in 2006–7, but he probably didn't have the pace or nip in this series as he did then. I thought we played him a lot better when he eventually played this time around, even though he got three quick wickets in Leeds. I was actually surprised he played ahead of Lee at Headingley and the Oval.

Michael Clarke

Born: 2 April 1981
Batting style: Right-handed
Bowling style: Slow left-arm orthodox

2009 Ashes Record

Matches	Innings	Not out	Runs	Highest score	Average	100s	50s	
5	8	1	448	136	64.00	2	2	

Matches	Overs	Runs	Wickets	Average	Runs per over	Best bowling	5 in an innings	10 in a match
5	19	75	1	75.00	3.94	1-12	0	0

Test Career Record (2004–9)

Matches	Innings	Not out	Runs	Highest score	Average	100s	50s	
52	84	10	3652	151	49.35	12	15	

Matches	Overs	Runs	Wickets	Average	Runs per over	Best bowling	5 in an innings	10 in a match
52	256.4	755	19	39.73	2.94	6-9	1	0

The Australian man of the series and a batsman who is very difficult to bowl to. He has changed his game a little bit since 2005, when he didn't do particularly well against the swinging ball. He played it much, much better this time and deserved to get three hundreds in the series. Probably didn't deserve to be on the losing side, and I think the most excited we got throughout the whole series was running him out on the last day at the Oval because we know how dangerous and awkward he can be. Looks like a future Australian captain.

Brad Haddin

Born: 23 October 1977
Batting style: Right-handed
Wicketkeeper

2009 Ashes Record

Matches	Innings	Not out	Runs	Highest score	Average	100s	50s
4	6	0	278	121	46.33	1	1

Test Career Record (2008–9)

Matches	Innings	Not out	Runs	Highest score	Average	100s	50s
19	32	2	1179	169	39.30	2	3

Had a very tough act to follow in Adam Gilchrist, but it looks like Australia have found a similar sort of player in Haddin. He comes at you hard from behind the stumps and when he bats, and again he was another Australian player to get a very good hundred at Cardiff. Very dangerous at number 7, and while it is impossible to replace Gilchrist, this bloke is as near as you can get to filling his shoes. I like the keeper to be a batsman who plays attacking shots, like Matt Prior does for us, and Haddin fits the bill.

Nathan Hauritz

Born: 18 October 1981
Batting style: Right-handed
Bowling style: Right-arm off-break

2009 Ashes Record

Matches	Innings	Not out	Runs	Highest score	Average	100s	50s	
3	3	1	45	24	22.50	0	0	

Matches	Overs	Runs	Wickets	Average	Runs per over	Best bowling	5 in an innings	10 in a match
3	103.2	321	10	32.10	3.10	3-63	0	0

Test Career Record (2004–9)

Matches	Innings	Not out	Runs	Highest score	Average	100s	50s	
7	9	1	117	41	14.62	0	0	

Matches	Overs	Runs	Wickets	Average	Runs per over	Best bowling	5 in an innings	10 in a match
7	271.2	773	24	32.20	2.84	3-16	0	0

Hauritz was another huge surprise to us because we watched him play in Australia's first tour match at Sussex and he didn't seem to be in any sort of rhythm, and it looked like we would be able to score quite freely off him. So we made it our aim to attack him, but that didn't work out because he bowled really well and proved worthy of his place as the spinner in the Australia side. Maybe Australia made their biggest mistake of the series in not playing Hauritz at the Oval. They will never be able to replace Shane Warne, but this guy can do a very good job for them.

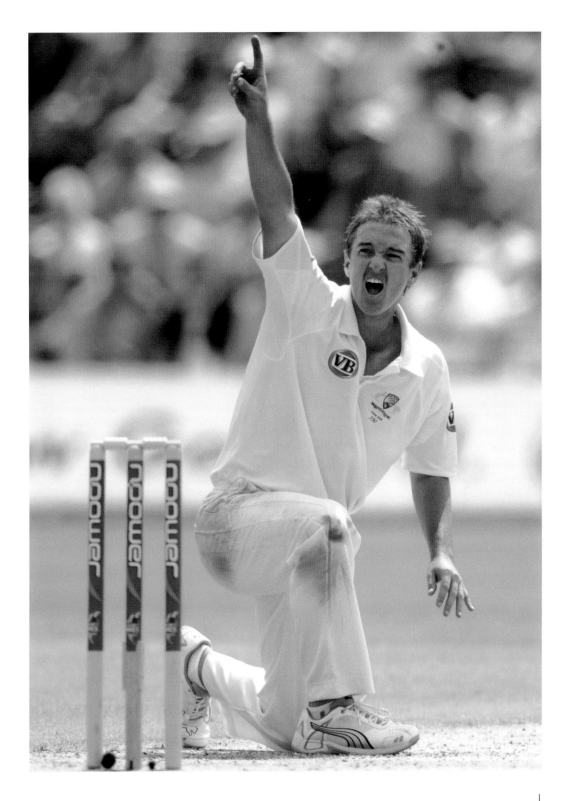

Ben Hilfenhaus

Born: 15 March 1983
Batting style: Right-handed
Bowling style: Right-arm fast-medium

2009 Ashes Record

Matches	Innings	Not out	Runs	Highest score	Average	100s	50s	
5	6	4	40	20	20.00	0	0	

Matches	Overs	Runs	Wickets	Average	Runs per over	Best bowling	5 in an innings	10 in a match
5	180.5	604	22	27.45	3.34	4-60	0	0

Test Career Record (2009–9)

Matches	Innings	Not out	Runs	Highest score	Average	100s	50s	
8	11	5	68	20	11.33	0	0	

Matches	Overs	Runs	Wickets	Average	Runs per over	Best bowling	5 in an innings	10 in a match
8	305.5	970	29	33.44	3.17	4-60	0	0

Another real workhorse for Australia, and someone who I am sure would pick up hundreds of wickets if he played county cricket because he just runs in all day and plonks it on a length again and again.

He was a bit of a surprise package because we expected Brett Lee to play until he hurt his side, and for Hilfenhaus not only to play but to take the wickets he did shocked us and just proved what consistency can do.

Phil Hughes

Born: 30 November 1988
Batting style: Left-handed
Bowling style: Right-arm off-break

2009 Ashes Record

Matches	Innings	Not out	Runs	Highest score	Average	100s	50s
2	3	0	57	36	19.00	0	0

Test Career Record (2009–9)

Matches	Innings	Not out	Runs	Highest score	Average	100s	50s
5	9	0	472	160	52.44	2	1

He is going to be a hugely successful Test cricketer despite the problems he had, which saw him dropped after the first two Tests. He just got unlucky really, with Steve Harmison working him over during the Lions match against Australia at Worcester, and then Andrew Flintoff bowling so well at him at Cardiff and Lord's.

It showed he has a chink in his armour at this stage in his career, which we were able to exploit, but he will come through that and go on to great heights. When he played county cricket for Middlesex I heard people saying he was the nearest thing they had ever seen to Brian Lara, and even though he is unorthodox, I can see him averaging above 50 in Test cricket. I'm sure we'll be having a lot of battles with Hughes in the years ahead.

Mike Hussey

Born: 27 May 1975
Batting style: Left-handed
Bowling style: Right-arm medium

2009 Ashes Record

Matches	Innings	Not out	Runs	Highest score	Average	100s	50s
5	8	0	276	121	34.50	1	2

Test Career Record (2005–9)

Matches	Innings	Not out	Runs	Highest score	Average	100s	50s
42	72	9	3317	182	52.65	10	16

Matches	Overs	Runs	Wickets	Average	Runs per over	Best bowling	5 in an innings	10 in a match
42	28	100	1	100.00	3.57	1–22	0	0

They call him 'Mr Cricket', and he is a batsman who has done it the hard way, in that he played so much county cricket and first-class cricket in Australia before he made his Test debut, in November 2005. His stats, particularly in his first year, when he averaged just under 76, are ridiculously good. Then to come in and average nearly 92 in his first Ashes series, in 2006–7, is amazing.

I think we bowled particularly well at Hussey. We made sure we didn't let him leave the ball, as he likes to do, but he deserved his century at the Oval. I am delighted he didn't get going before that because he is a very difficult player to remove once he is in.

Mitchell Johnson

Born: 2 November 1981
Batting style: Left-handed
Bowling style: Left-arm fast

2009 Ashes Record

Matches	Innings	Not out	Runs	Highest score	Average	100s	50s	
5	6	0	105	63	17.50	0	1	

Matches	Overs	Runs	Wickets	Average	Runs per over	Best bowling	5 in an innings	10 in a match
5	162.1	651	20	32.55	4.01	5-69	1	0

Test Career Record (2007-9)

Matches	Innings	Not out	Runs	Highest score	Average	100s	50s	
26	34	8	799	123 not out	30.73	1	4	

Matches	Overs	Runs	Wickets	Average	Runs per over	Best bowling	5 in an innings	10 in a match
26	1047.3	3284	114	28.80	3.13	8-61	3	1

The Australian player I had most battles with. Always gave me a lot of chirp when I came out to bat and showed a lot of aggression on the field. His record shows that he is a fantastic bowler, but he struggled a little in the first couple of matches in the Ashes. Our media played their part in making him feel under pressure, but he came through that with flying colours. The best thing for me was that, again, when we had a beer after the final Test he was one of the nicest men you could wish to meet, and he was recognised for his endeavours when he became the ICC player of the year in October.

Simon Katich

Born: 21 August 1975
Batting style: Left-handed
Bowling style: Left-arm chinaman

2009 Ashes Record

Matches	Innings	Not out	Runs	Highest score	Average	100s	50s		
5	8	0	341	122	42.62	1	1		

Matches	Overs	Runs	Wickets	Average	Runs per over	Best bowling	5 in an innings	10 in a match
5	10	27	0	–	2.70	–	0	0

Test Career Record (2001–9)

Matches	Innings	Not out	Runs	Highest score	Average	100s	50s		
43	74	5	2990	157	43.33	8	16		

Matches	Overs	Runs	Wickets	Average	Runs per over	Best bowling	5 in an innings	10 in a match
43	153.1	560	18	31.11	3.65	6-65	1	0

For me a very difficult player to bowl to. Has an unorthodox technique but knows his game well and doesn't play shots that he doesn't need to. Katich is a batsman I will have to do my homework on for when we next meet because I struggled to contain him, let alone get him out. He's turned himself from a number 5 who did not make too much of an impact against us in 2005 into a quality opening batsman. I rate him very highly.

Graham Manou

Born: 23 April 1979
Batting style: Right-handed
Wicketkeeper

2009 Ashes Record

Matches	Innings	Not out	Runs	Highest score	Average	100s	50s
1	2	1	21	13 not out	21.00	0	0

I think I broke his finger in his first Test innings at Edgbaston. There was chaos at the start of that match when Brad Haddin broke his own finger in the warm-up and Manou was thrown in at the last minute for his Test debut. Jimmy got him in the end with an absolute pearler that swung in and then nipped away, so there was not much he could do about that. Didn't really speak to the bloke at all.

Marcus North

Born: 28 July 1979
Batting style: **Left-handed**
Bowling style: **Right-arm off-break**

2009 Ashes Record

Matches	Innings	Not out	Runs	Highest score	Average	100s	50s		
5	8	1	367	125 not out	52.42	2	1		

Matches	Overs	Runs	Wickets	Average	Runs per over	Best bowling	5 in an innings	10 in a match
5	67.3	204	4	51.00	3.02	4-98	0	0

Test Career Record (2009-9)

Matches	Innings	Not out	Runs	Highest score	Average	100s	50s		
7	12	1	527	125 not out	47.90	3	1		

Matches	Overs	Runs	Wickets	Average	Runs per over	Best bowling	5 in an innings	10 in a match
7	105.3	302	6	50.33	2.86	4-98	0	0

Probably the biggest surprise to me in the series. I'd played against him in county cricket before and I thought he was a candidate for lbw when the ball swung. That proved simply wrong because he looked very strong and had tightened up his technique considerably. He was a powerful driver and puller, which you need to be in England. Luckily, Graeme Swann got him out a few times and bowled fantastically well at him, but his hundred at Cardiff set the tone for him and he went on to have a really good series, having not been guaranteed his place at the start of the summer.

Peter Siddle

Born: 25 November 1984
Batting style: Right-handed
Bowling style: Right-arm fast-medium

2009 Ashes Record

Matches	Innings	Not out	Runs	Highest score	Average	100s	50s		
5	6	1	91	35	18.20	0	0		

Matches	Overs	Runs	Wickets	Average	Runs per over	Best bowling	5 in an innings	10 in a match
5	161.4	616	20	30.80	3.81	5-21	1	0

Test Career Record (2008-9)

Matches	Innings	Not out	Runs	Highest score	Average	100s	50s		
12	18	4	197	35	14.07	0	0		

Matches	Overs	Runs	Wickets	Average	Runs per over	Best bowling	5 in an innings	10 in a match
12	472.5	1418	49	28.93	2.99	5-21	2	0

Very fiery character who I had an early run-in with when there was a little shoulder barge between us in Cardiff. But a real workhorse and tryer and someone you want to have in your team because he never gives up and doesn't stop running in. An example perhaps of how statistics sometimes do lie: the Aussies had the leading wicket-takers, runmakers and century-makers in the series, but we ended up winning it because we seized the big moments and the big sessions. That's key.

Siddle bowled us out on that first day at Headingley and was someone we found very hard to face throughout the series.

Shane Watson

Born: 17 June 1981
Batting style: Right-handed
Bowling style: Right-arm fast-medium

2009 Ashes Record

Matches	Innings	Not out	Runs	Highest score	Average	100s	50s	
3	5	0	240	62	48.00	0	3	

Matches	Overs	Runs	Wickets	Average	Runs per over	Best bowling	5 in an innings	10 in a match
3	8	49	0	–	6.12	–	0	0

Test Career Record (2005–9)

Matches	Innings	Not out	Runs	Highest score	Average	100s	50s	
11	18	0	497	78	27.61	0	4	

Matches	Overs	Runs	Wickets	Average	Runs per over	Best bowling	5 in an innings	10 in a match
11	169.4	547	14	39.07	3.22	4-42	0	0

Came in after Phil Hughes had a tough couple of Tests. The sort of character who can get under people's skin on the pitch and is difficult to bowl to, and he scored consistent half-centuries when he came in as an opener from the third Test onwards.

He is someone who seemed to bring most aggression out of the England bowlers, and I think everyone had a few words with him at some point during the series. But what summed up the Australians for me was meeting Watson in the changing room after the final day of the series. He was a really nice bloke who was great to talk to, and that sums up the Australian attitude. Uncompromising on the pitch but very friendly and interesting off it.

Acknowledgements

First of all, I would like to thank my parents, Carole and Chris, and their other halves Nick and Miche, for all their support. Without their understanding, as well as that of the rest of my family and friends, none of my success would have been possible.

Warm thanks are due to Craig Sackfield for his wise advice and expert guidance.

I am hugely indebted to Paul Newman. Without his professionalism, this book would simply not have happened. It has been a pleasure to work with him.

I'd also like to acknowledge the England players, staff and management who all worked so tirelessly to make the leap to being an Ashes-winning team again.

Finally, I would like to thank the team at Hodder & Stoughton, including Roddy Bloomfield and Sarah Hammond, as well as Trish Burgess and Bob Vickers, for all their work in bringing this book together so quickly after the wonderful day that England won the Ashes.

Photographic Acknowledgements

The author and publisher would like to thank the following for permission to reproduce photographs:

Barry Batchelor/PA, page 47; Hamish Blair/Getty Images, pages 56 left, 63, 82, 96, 99, 101, 191; Philip Brown, pages 2, 27 right, 39, 48, 49 left & right, 51, 52, 53, 56 right, 60 left & right, 64 left & right, 65, 68 above, 70, 73 above, 79 left & right, 81, 83 left, 86, 90, 92 left, 94, 106 above & below, 109, 114, 118, 122, 132/133, 135, 137, 139, 141, 143, 147, 149, 151, 157, 161, 163, 165, 169, 171, 173, 175, 177, 179, 181, 183, 187, 189; John Buckle/Empics Sport, page 123 left; Neville Chadwick Photography, page 21 below right; Gareth Copley/PA, pages 45, 88, 111, 159; Adam Davey/Empics Sport, page 120; Patrick Eagar, pages 54 below, 62, 66, 71, 73 below, 75, 85, 92 right, 102 above & below, 110, 112, 113, 123 right, 185; Mike Egerton/Empics Sport, pages 33, 155; Stu Forster/Getty Images, pages 29, 30, 31 right, 32, 89; Andrew Fosker, pages 115, 121; Paul Gilham/Getty Images, page 116; Robert Hallam/Rex Features, page 17; Richard Heathcote/Getty Images, pages 100 right, 105 left; Scott Heavey/Action Images, pages 69, 72, 119; Julian Herbert/Getty Images, page 37; Mike Hewitt/Getty Images, page 74; Colin Howe/Colbeck Photography, page 15; Matthew Impey/PA, page 35; Saeed Khan/AFP/Getty Images, page 27 left; Ian Kington/AFP/Getty Images, page 68 below; Matthew Lewis/Getty Images, page 21 left; Graham Morris, pages 19, 21 above right, 67, 76, 83 right, 97 right, 103, 124, 153; Phil O'Brien/Empics Sport, pages 6/7; Martin Rickett/PA, page 26; Clive Rose/Getty Images, pages 24, 57 above & below; Tom Shaw/Getty Images, pages 34, 42/43, 87, 95, 105 right, 125, 126, 167; Bob Thomas/Getty Images, page 9; Paul Thomas/AP/PA, pages 31 left, 40; Mark Thompson/Getty Images, page 23; William West/AFP/Getty Images, pages 55, 59, 100 left, 117 left & right; Kirsty Wrigglesworth/AP/PA, page 145; Andrew Yates/AFP/Getty Images, pages 54 above, 97 left.

All other photographs are from private collections.